BRITAIN

A WORLD BY ITSELF

BRITAIN

A WORLD BY ITSELF

REFLECTIONS ON THE LANDSCAPE
BY EMINENT BRITISH WRITERS

PHOTOGRAPHS BY

PAUL WAKEFIELD

BROCKHAMPTON PRESS
LONDON

This edition published 1998 by Brockhampton Press Ltd.
a member of Hodder Headline PLC Group

ISBN 1 86019 8260

Photographs copyright © Paul Wakefield 1984
Text copyright © Ronald Blythe 1984
© Melvyn Bragg 1984
© George Mackay Brown 1984
© John Fowles 1984
© Geoffrey Grigson 1984
© Ted Hughes 1984
© Jan Morris 1984
© Iain Crichton Smith 1984
© Edward Storey 1984
© R. S. Thomas 1984
© Richard Williamson 1984

Printed at Oriental Press, Dubai, U.A.E.

CONTENTS

THE CONTRIBUTORS

RONALD BLYTHE, poet, novelist, essayist and critic, is perhaps best known as the author of *Akenfield,* a classic portrait of village life in East Anglia, where he himself lives and writes.

MELVYN BRAGG, writer and broadcaster, is Head of Arts at London Weekend Television and editor and presenter of the South Bank Show. Several of his novels are set in the Lake District, about which he has also written in *Land of the Lakes.* Now living in London, he escapes to his native Cumbria as often as he can.

GEORGE MACKAY BROWN's writing has its centre in images and themes from Orkney, where he has always lived. His most recent novel, *Time in a Red Coat,* is about war and man's chances of survival. He is currently preparing new books of poems and a book of long stories.

JOHN FOWLES achieved worldwide acclaim for his second novel, *The French Lieutenant's Woman,* published in 1969, and since then has consolidated his reputation with *The Ebony Tower* and *Daniel Martin.* In 1979 he wrote the text for *The Tree,* published by Aurum Press. He lives in Dorset.

GEOFFREY GRIGSON is a well-known poet, literary critic and anthologist. His lifelong interest in the countryside is reflected in his writings, and his compilations include many books on the English landscape. Born in Cornwall, he now lives in Wiltshire.

TED HUGHES has published many collections of poetry, among them *Moortown,* a verse journal of his experiences of farming in Devon, where he lives.

JAN MORRIS, who is half Welsh, has a home in the Black Mountains. Historian as well as travel-writer, she collaborated with Paul Wakefield on the picture essay *Wales: The First Place,* and in 1984 Oxford University Press published her major study of the country, *The Matter of Wales.*

FRANKLYN PERRING has been General Secretary of the Royal Society for Nature Conservation since 1979. In that capacity he writes regularly on conservation issues in *Natural World,* the RSNC magazine. He is co-author of the *Atlas of the British Flora* and has written or edited ten other botanical books.

IAIN CRICHTON SMITH is described in *The Penguin Book of Scottish Verse* as 'the best Scottish poet now writing in English'. Born on the island of Lewis, he now lives and writes in Taynuilt, Argyll.

EDWARD STOREY was born in the Isle of Ely, Cambridgeshire. He has made a particular study of the Fen country, about which he has written four books, and is the author of *A Right to Song: A Life of John Clare.* He is also a poet, librettist and regular broadcaster on radio and television.

R. S. THOMAS is a native of Wales and was vicar of the parish in which he now lives. He has published a dozen collections of poetry for which he has won various awards, including the Queen's Gold Medal for Poetry in 1964. His latest collection of poems, *Between Here and Now,* was published in 1981.

RICHARD WILLIAMSON, son of Henry Williamson, is, like his father, passionately involved with natural history. Author of numerous wildlife articles, he has also written three books, one an account of Kingley Vale, the oldest yew forest in Europe, of which he is warden. With his wife Anne he is currently preparing the definitive biography of his father.

A
DEVON RIVER

TED HUGHES

Nymet

No map or Latin ever

Netted one deity from this river.
TAW meant simply *water*.
What were her true names
When she poured these pools from her ewer

And gave her breast to the strange hunters
Who followed the dying Mastodon
That came down through Belstone?
How did they name her

When she drew their offerings and prayer
Into her tunnel water
With the brother-blood of heron and otter
As into cave-womb rock?

THE RIVER TAW AT SKAIGH WARREN, DEVON

THE RIVER TAW NEAR ROWDEN MOOR

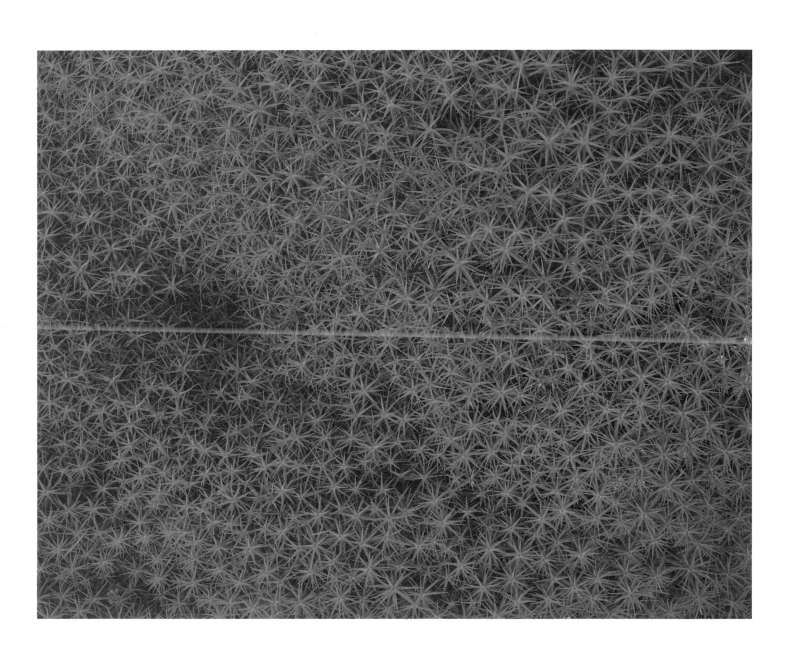

CORD-MOSS NEAR ROWDEN

Then with yellow smoky nettle pollen
And the first thorn's confetti
Crushed the May bridegroom's
Head into her flood?

Afterwards, she bore him, without fail,
All summer a splendour
Of eel-wreaths and a glut of white peal,
And right on through summer and winter the glow-cold

Sea-new salmon. Her names and her coombes
Deepened together: 'Our Bride, Our Mother, Our Nurse'.
Where is she now?
A fairy

Drowned in the radio-active Irish Sea.
Blood-donor
To the South-West Water Authority.
Her womb's been requisitioned

For the cloacal flux, the privy curse
Of the Express Dairy Cheese Factory –
'Biggest in Europe'.
A miasma

Mourns on the town bridge, at odd hours,
Over her old home, now her grave.
That's her.
She rots

But still stirs – a nightly, dewy spectre,
Nameless revenant
In her grave-clothes, resurrected
By her maternal despair

For her dying fish. She wipes their lips
Of the stuff that weeps
From her curdled dug since it became
The fistula of a thousand farms. That's her –

The milk-herd's daily discharge of detergent,
The sheep-flock's and the beef-herd's purgation,
Ferment of silage in her every vein,
The earthen town's overkill of hygiene –

And so we have christened her: Sewer of all Sewers.

But she is that Celtic apparition,
The fatal vision, who comes near the end of stories:
The Washer at the Ford.
The death-rags that she washes and washes are ours.

During the last forty years the Water Authorities have ravaged Britain's rivers in their quest for greater flood control. Thousands of miles of streams and rivers have been dredged and bankside herbs, shrubs and trees removed, turning winding wildernesses into straight, dull, sterile aqueducts in which no wildlife can survive. Simultaneously the increased drainage has led adjacent farmers to plough up old meadows, removing hedges and copses. In the process whole landscapes have been destroyed, and some of our most loved wild creatures have been lost from large areas of the countryside. Herons which once nested in the copses and fed on frogs in marshy river margins have gone from many valleys, while the shy otter, which until the mid-1950s was common along overgrown streams and shaded river banks in every county of Britain, is now absent from almost the whole of England and Wales.

The initial decline of the otter was almost certainly due to organochlorine pesticides, particularly dieldrin, the use of which at the end of the 1950s began contaminating waterways and the fish upon which the otters depended. But their failure to recover when dieldrin was banned was due to the fact that in the 1960s and 1970s most of their habitats had been disturbed or destroyed.

In 1981 the Wildlife and Countryside Act imposed on Water Authorities the duty to further the conservation of the flora and fauna so far as this is consistent with their prime duty of flood control and land drainage. Yet the destruction still continues.

Otters and other water-dependent creatures will only survive in Britain if they are given priority on some water courses. Does every stream and river have to be canalized? And even on those where work is essential, cannot secluded stretches be left untouched or one bank remain uncleared? From these refuges the habitat could be recolonized, after the drag-line has passed, by native plants and animals.

There are encouraging signs that this is beginning to happen: Severn-Trent Water Authority has left riverside trees and persuaded farmers to manage them as sources of timber or firewood so that falling branches do not impede the water flow; the South West, on one of its rivers, has created a small marshy area and cut off a meander to leave a wooded islet suitable for otter cover. But is this too little, too late, to repair the havoc already created?

The Wildlife and Countryside Act is a challenge to Water Authorities: from now on they must all take a responsible and constructive attitude to nature conservation and carry out their duties in such a way that they create as many habitats as they destroy, leaving the countryside they move through as rich or richer in wildlife than before they came. They must also appreciate that their work should serve the whole community and not just the landowners, who for several decades have used political pressure to put through drainage schemes – largely paid for from the public purse – thereby increasing the value of the land for their private gain while depriving the public of a priceless landscape.

THE RIVER TAW AT BELSTONE CLEAVE

THE CHESIL BANK

JOHN FOWLES

I seldom go to the Chesil Bank without feeling faintly frustrated. Was ever a landscape so ridiculously narrow and long, so determined to thwart the visitor? It looks a nonsense on maps: a primitive long-handled stone axe or knobkerrie, the head formed by the Portland peninsula – the only thing to which, until quite recently, its southern end was connected.

Walking the Chesil is for masochists only. Half a mile on the shingle is worse than two miles on solid land. Understanding it – that is, trying to plough through the endless shifting pebbles of professional geographical and geological theory as to why it behaves as it does, indeed why it exists at all, is almost as arduous, at least to the poor layman. This most strandlike of strands breaks all the rules. Everywhere else in the Channel, beach material is carried eastward; here it is westward, and lightest furthest. Its smallest shingle goes to the north-west, its largest to the south-east, and with such obsessive exactitude that an old Chesil hand, landing in a thick fog on any of its eighteen miles, knows just where he is by pebble size. But there it is, one of the great wonders of English landscape, a flagrant anomaly in that of generally cliffed Dorset. The old notion that it all blew up in one night can sometimes seem the most plausible.

THE CHESIL BANK, DORSET, LOOKING WEST

THE CHESIL, LOOKING EAST

The sharp shelves of the beach, its undertow and rogue waves, mean that only fools ignore the warnings against swimming. The nearest lifeboat, at Lyme Regis, has almost every year to make the twelve or fifteen mile journey to the Bank; another swimmer has learnt the hard way – only too often, the final way. The onshore beach anglers are wiser, and far more picturesque, in their scattered groups, with their long rods and even longer vigils for the bass and other fish they are after.

The Chesil is rich in an older human history. This was once a distinctly lawless area; and all its villages, Burton Bradstock, Swyre, Puncknowle, Abbotsbury, Langton Herring, East Fleet and Chickerell, were guilty. An eighteenth-century traveller said that all the inhabitants of Abbotsbury, 'including the Vicar', were smugglers, thieves and wreck-plunderers. They evolved also a special form of fishing, seine-netting, and a special double-ended fishing-boat, the lerret. Nets were rowed round shoals of fish such as mackerel and sprats and then hauled in by teams on shore. At Burton the old cry of 'Vish strayen!' (fish straying into inshore shoals) or the sound of the mackerel horn would at once bring normal life to an abrupt stop, as everyone flocked to the beach. These fishermen were highly superstitious. They never shot a seine on Sundays, or harmed a seagull (for these held drowned sailors' souls). Their lerrets always carried a holed (or holy) stone at bow and stern for luck; if this failed, and the boat was bewitched, a dead mackerel was stuck with pins and brought aboard. Holed stones were used by the smugglers also, as sinking-weights on their tubs of brandy.

For nearly half its eighteen-mile length, the Chesil runs side by side with an inland lagoon, the Fleet, which varies in width from half a mile to a long stone's throw, a mere hundred yards. It has only one narrow outlet to the sea, and so is very shallow; halfheartedly tidal, with flats of rich organic silt, its western end more brackish than fully salt. This makes it a great haven and larder for aquatic birds. Much of its inner shore can be walked. The sheltered backslope of the Chesil opposite has low vegetation, salt-tolerant plants that find a living there. Its eastern half is not quite deserted; here and there you may see ramshackle huts made of driftwood, like fragments from a set for *Peter*

Grimes. The western end is lonelier, for it is one of the oldest bird sanctuaries in Britain; its famous swannery goes back to medieval times. The mute swans there breed colonially, in the charge of a swanherd, and are much less aggressive than the solitary-nesting pairs of the normal river bank.

I was beside the Fleet at Herbury at the end of April, watching migrating parties of bar-tailed godwit, the males in their rich rust-red breeding plumage, come in over the Chesil and land to wash and feed. Some early terns also; grey and ringed plover, dunlin, a turnstone, oystercatchers, shelduck, a small flock of red-breasted merganser, swimming in their strange flattened way, like would-be torpedoes, after the flounders and eels they feed on here. Finally I heard one of the loneliest and most haunting of all bird cries. Whimbrel; seven came in, and landed beside the godwits. It was a very calm evening, and I watched this beautiful assemblage in the pooled reflection of a greeny-yellow field of rape inland across the water.

Not all bird-watching experiences at the Fleet are quite so classical. A few weeks earlier I was watching two swans fly in to land on a meadow, where sheep grazed. Then suddenly a quite ridiculous flash of shocking pink also flew into my field of vision. It landed some fifty yards from where the swans were, then minced delicately across the grass to them for all the world like some effete ponce coming to make a proposition. The Fleet evidently has three-star rating for *Phoenicopterus ruber,* as they are quite often seen there when they escape. A wild South American flamingo in an English sheep-meadow belongs much more to Lewis Carroll than ornithology.

Abbotsbury is the undisputed queen of the Chesil: one of the most beautiful villages in west Dorset, saved from having become a popular seaside resort by the Chesil itself, or its danger as a bathing place. One's first view, coming high from the west, of the lyncheted hill crowned by St Catherine's Chapel, with the Fleet and the Chesil stretching vastly away beyond, is one of the most beautiful in England. I have seen it in many different lights and moods. It is always fresh, verdant, acutely pleasing; a slightly fairy-tale domain spread at one's feet. The 600-foot chalk downs that overlook the Chesil are dense with the tumuli, lynchets, trackways, stone circles and enclosures of earlier

THE FLEET AND CHESIL BANK FROM WEARS HILL

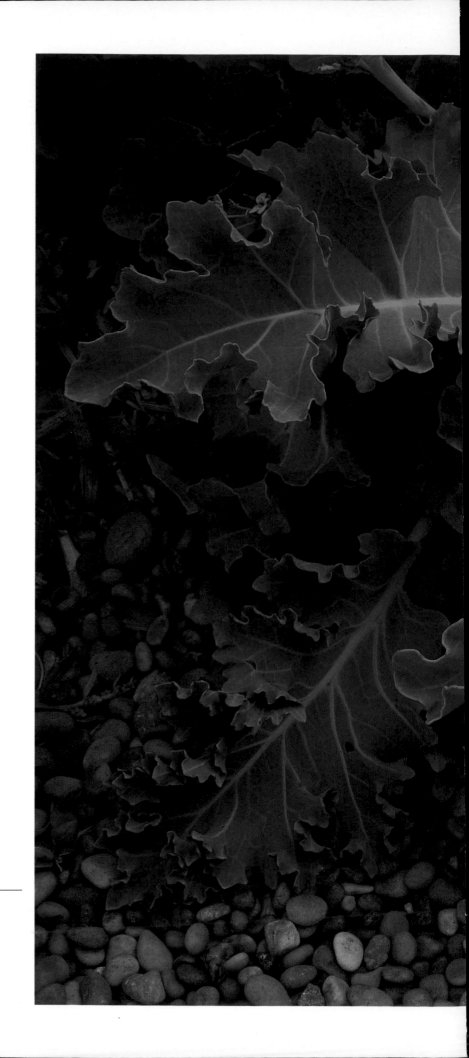

SEAKALE ON THE CHESIL

mankind. This steep green backdrop is an essential part of the magic by the sea below.

Abbotsbury can satisfy the botanist and gardener, too. Its Subtropical Gardens, in a wood only a few hundred yards behind the Bank, grow many very rare plants and trees. Founded by the first Countess of Ilchester in 1765, a little way back from her now ruined summer villa directly above the Chesil, the gardens lie within the vital belt of warmer winter temperature afforded by the sea, where frosts are very rare. That is why such splendid palm trees and camellias and magnolias survive there. The most famous is a huge *Magnolia campbellii,* now sixty foot tall, and a breathtaking sight with its enormous pink tulip-flowers in full bloom – almost as unreal, or surreal, as the flamingo.

From the Subtropical Gardens you have only to stroll a short distance to see a very different flora – that of the backslope of the Chesil Bank itself. Many rare native plants such as the sea pea and sea kale, the yellow horned-poppy and shrubby sea-blite, survive this difficult environment. One of the most charming – and commonest – is the scurvy-grass, *Cochlearia danica.* Its myriad tiny flowers mist the bare shingle with an ethereal lilac-tinged ashy light in spring. Closer to, you must kneel; they are like alpine plants. Here as elsewhere the Chesil is lined at the back with groves of tamarisk. Nearby grows another 'foreigner', the Duke of Argyll's tea-plant, a favourite shrub of mine because of the colour of its newly opened flowers. One *Hortus* I have describes *Lycium chinense* as 'dull lilac purple'; which deserves a suit for libel.

Its presence is apt, because the aesthetic essence, the deepest appeal of the Chesil Bank is to me oriental. It calls to that ancient Chinese delight in nature and landscape, to that metaphysical respect for the simple we associate with Zen Buddhism. It is above all an elemental place, made of sea, shingle and sky, its dominant sound always that of waves on moving stone; from the great surf and pounding 'ground seas' of sou'westers, to the delicate laps and back-gurglings of the rare dead calms. That zone between the dry, bleached pebbles above the waves and the wetted ones within their reach, where their colours come alive – 'where they flower', as an old fisherman once put it to me – can become hypnotic. One walks with head bowed, oblivious to all but that constantly rewashed world at one's feet. Most of the pebbles are of

Cretaceous chert and flint, but pebbles of much more ancient stones from Devon, even Cornwall, appear. However, the Chesil was always a ferocious trapper of sailing-ships, and countless of them carried stone as ballast; modern geologists treat exotic 'erratics' here with caution. The beach has airier beauties; a phenomenon I have seen once or twice in misty conditions is the Chesil in the sky, a kind of aerial glow that continues long after the actual strand disappears from view. By an exquisite illusion it becomes a dim golden ghost or halo over its vanished real self below.

I can see the Chesil from where I live, but I do not feel attached to it in a literary way; it is not 'my' country, fond though I am of it. As with all special landscapes nowadays, celebrating it in old-fashioned terms raises ethical problems. If the Chesil and the Fleet and their hinterland need anything, it is practical preserving and guarding, not descriptive prose. They are in any case their own prose – and poetry – and in a language infinitely more subtle and rich than words. Celebration entails a certain blindness, a seeing only the good side; what mercifully remains, not what encroaches and threatens. I have not mentioned the seeping of Weymouth north-westwards, nor the increasing 'leisure use' of the East Fleet. I have not mentioned that Herbury, where I watched the birds, is also a proposed nuclear power station site – on the shelf at the moment, but not certainly dropped for ever. I have not mentioned the commonest (in both senses) sign of life on the backslope of the Bank – the foul scatter of plastic rubbish, blown over from where it washes up after being thrown overboard by Channel shipping; nor a grim reality of the green downs that overlook the Fleet and Chesil. These days they are endless 'improved' grassland, almost all their wild flowers gone. The great sarsen stones of the Neolithic long-barrow in the hills behind Abbotsbury, the Grey Mare and her Colts, are only too fittingly funereal: they stand among ecologically dead fields.

So I cannot *only* celebrate the Chesil. If I acted in its best interest, I suspect I should say it is not worth the visit. But alas, it is. All I can pray for is what I am myself, the loving visitor; and the good sense and decency in human affairs that remains as thin – and sometimes as improbable – a barrier against our worse and greedier selves as the Chesil Bank itself, against the destroying sea.

REEDS ON THE FLEET

THE SWANNERY, ABBOTSBURY

From the saltmarshes round Britain's shores to the tops of the Scottish mountains, our wildlife is being destroyed to the point where the once common is now rare, much that was rare is now extinct, and certain habitats have disappeared from whole counties or regions.

Since 1949, 95 per cent of our hay meadows have been destroyed; 80 per cent of chalk and limestone grasslands have been converted to arable or 'improved'; 50-60 per cent of lowland heaths have been ploughed up or have become scrubbed over through lack of grazing; 30-50 per cent of ancient broad-leaved woods have been converted to conifers or grubbed up to make more farmland; 50 per cent of lowland wetlands have been drained; and probably 30 per cent of upland heaths and grassland have been afforested, drained or treated with fertilizers.

To these man-made losses must be added those inevitably produced by the forces of nature which are constantly eroding the landscape, most particularly round the coast. The cliffs on either side of Lyme Regis on the border of Devon and Dorset and on the south coast of the Isle of Wight are geologically unstable and constantly slip into the sea, taking grassland, scrub and woodland with them. The coastlines of the Holderness in east Yorkshire, of north Lincolnshire and east Suffolk are being cut into by currents which sweep southwards down the North Sea.

But however great the losses due to nature, she, unlike man, always compensates. The crumbling cliffs of the east coast have been deposited further south as the spit of Spurn Head, the sandy beaches of Gibraltar Point and the complex of shingle ridges round Orfordness – each now an area rich in wildlife, embracing nature reserves of national importance. On the south coast the chalk and limestone cliffs of Beer and Lyme have been carried by the action of the waves up the Channel to contribute to the Chesil Bank.

The lesson is clear. We too must learn to follow nature's habitats to compensate for the horrendous losses of the last thirty-five years. Ecologists now have sufficient understanding of the interrelationships of plants and animals to make it possible to build simple communities such as water's edge and old grassland wherever opportunities arise. Progress has already been made. Gravel pits at the edge of expanding towns such as Milton Keynes and Peterborough – artefacts of their construction – have been planned and planted to add enjoyment of wildlife to their leisure facilities. A few local authorities, such as Basildon in Essex, are sowing wild flower seeds on the banks of new roads to gladden the eye and encourage the butterflies. This practice could be adopted on new roads throughout the country; likewise, when boundary hedges are planted they could be composed of a mixture of shrubs to provide food and shelter for birds and insects.

By positive planning and management many thousands of acres of water, grassland and hedgerow could be transformed into wildlife habitats which, though never entirely replacing what we have destroyed, would ensure that the sounds, scents and sights of nature will continue to be a vivid part of living in Britain.

THE CHESIL BANK NEAR ABBOTSBURY

THE WILTSHIRE DOWNS

GEOFFREY GRIGSON

By accident and by choice I have lived for most of my life in landscape of two kinds, a shut landscape and an open one, the landscape of east Cornwall and the landscape of north Wiltshire, on the edge of downland and Salisbury Plain. The Cornish landscape belongs to childhood, the Wiltshire landscape to maturity, and different as they are, I have discovered in them a common affective element.

My Cornwall was much divided, deep valleyed country, through which roads were overgrown lanes still of a narrowness more suitable for pack-animals. These deep water-mint valleys or coombes – one of them began in our steep-sided garden – twisted to the sea, which can never be far away in Cornwall, and is suddenly encountered in openings between cliffs.

My Cornish landscape is a secret one, though villages and churches are close to each other; my Wiltshire landscape is an open one, the villages far apart.

Going back to Cornwall and its secretiveness, which I seldom do, I am rather horrified – if that isn't too big a word – to find in my old love for such an environment more of an inherited, historical character, less of a personal character than I like. From a reading lately of the first volume of Maurice Cranston's reconsideration of Jean-Jacques Rousseau, I realize how very much

THE DOWNS NEAR BARBURY CASTLE, WILTSHIRE

Rousseau's formulated preference in surrounding landscape has determined our own. Rousseau, that new European sensibility, with his sparkling eye, was all for mountain, crag, rock, waterfall, storm, for the involuted and convoluted. He wrote, when he was living below the Alps at Chambéry, in the Savoy, that 'Flat country, however beautiful it might be, has never seemed beautiful to me'. And here am I rejecting the Cornish miniature version of Rousseau's preference, if not plumping, exactly and totally, for the opposite.

My discovery of Wiltshire of the plain, half a century ago, led me to some degree of anti-romantic apostasy, of anti-Rousseauism. It began with a walk – a weekend escape out of London – from a station near Devizes, over sheep downland, to Avebury; from which I remember, not so much enigmatic standing stones, as a width of sky and slope and view, to an accompaniment, as it happened, of sheep-bells.

Lighten our darkness, lighten our secretiveness.

My apostasy was gradual, and has remained incomplete. I first came to live in Wiltshire, not long after, in a romantic or sub-Rousseauistic situation, under an escarpment, embossed with the velvet of tree clumps, a highway for moons full or crescent in the mode and the mood of Samuel Palmer whom I wrote about when he was still more or less unknown. But nowadays it is up to the downland that I go. I think to claim that this undramatic openness of landscape (which is rare for England) has 'influenced my writing' might be specious. Perhaps what can be claimed genuinely in that regard is becoming associated with a new landscape more or less in harmony with a discovered or recognized self. Or is it specious to say that in width each of us, as writers especially, may find a mental opening and growing up, a deprovincialization of interests, a rejection of a cosy, dangerous hiding away?

Anyhow, the affective element I valued and found in different ways, different degrees both in that secret Cornish milieu and the open Wiltshire milieu, was – and how old-fashioned a word it seems now – loneliness or solitude. In Cornwall car-parks have become too close, too ubiquitous for a genuineness of solitude such as I could find and feel once in a narrow water-mint slad visited by no one except myself, and a farmer in search of his heifers. In Wiltshire sunlight gleams off cars by the hundred parked at Avebury or Stonehenge, notices say 'Tank crossing', dogs from the town are being exercised, parents and children are playing with metal detectors, motor cycles rev and roar and slide along green tracks, red hang-gliders are floating into vales. But it remains country in which selective solitude is more possible.

In general, though, how is a necessary selective solitude to be maintained, without social affront? Improved agriculture eliminates poppies. Who is to tell farmers to do less well in the interests of 'spiritual' requirement?

A solution seems impossible, now that we have so increased our numbers, our means of transport, and our general destructiveness. I recommend one way of discovering what we have lost, and are still losing. Turn from plate to plate by William Daniell in the four volumes of *A Voyage round Great Britain* (1825) and compare a headland, say, or a harbour landscape which Daniell depicted for its charms in that era of Wellington and Waterloo and Wordsworth and Constable, with its present appearance smothered in houses precisely for love of a view which the smothering has destroyed.

Sitting and talking not so long ago with a Polperro fisherman (at least I suppose he still fished), and looking down on the quays, I discussed Polperro of my childhood as a place still of semi-solitude, compared with Polperro where we have to push through the alleys past gift shops. 'Well,' he said, 'you had it all your own way. Now they're having their share.' Unanswerable. No solution, no general solution.

Certainly Wiltshire – downland Wiltshire, which is the greater part of this ancient area – is going to retain a fair degree of emptiness and visible distance, in spite of the cars. Emptiness more or less is certainly going to survive in those great tracts which won't be controlled for ever by the War Department. I look forward to the day when the army camps in sight of Stonehenge will be pulled down, leaving downland Wiltshire a fair chance of entire renewal, if only because no other conglomerates of building and habitation are going to find cause for existence across what remains, on the whole, as for the last six thousand years, a vast sheep-walk.

Well protected antiquities add to the pleasures of this loneliness in time

STONE CIRCLE, AVEBURY

NETTLES AND THISTLEDOWN, FYFIELD DOWN

SWEET CHESTNUTS, SAVERNAKE FOREST

and in space. If you cut across the downland from prehistoric Avebury to medieval and modern Devizes you cut through Wansdyke – Woden's Dyke, the ditch and rampart of the high god of the Anglo-Saxons. Near this point on the dyke, on 11 June 1613, a Wiltshire clergyman, George Ferobe, made his shepherd parishioners perform a masque before Queen Anne, consort of James I, on her return from Bath to London. It included mention of 'the wide, wild houseless downs'. That is a good phrase. They are still wide, still wild more or less, and still more or less without houses. For the values of loneliness I like to think they will remain so – probably – for another 370 years; or another 6000 years.

The majority of the low hills which shape the landscape of south and east England are made of chalk, forming distinctive rounded downs and wolds. Until three hundred years ago their three million acres were mostly covered in short, herb-rich turf, the product of centuries of close grazing by millions of sheep. Today only 100,000 acres (3 per cent) remain, and much of that is threatened by human activity – or lack of it. Grazing sheep keep coarse grasses under control and allow the growth of small and attractive wild flowers. When grazing stops, even temporarily, tall vigorous grasses such as upright brome take over, eliminating low-growing, less competitive species. Longer neglect leads to invasion by woody shrubs, and eventually the grassland disappears beneath a dense thicket of hawthorn or dogwood.

Intensification of agriculture may be equally destructive. The use of selective herbicides, the application of artificial fertilizers and the sowing of commercial grasses in the wild turf all contribute to eliminating the majority of wild flowers. But, since the Second World War, it is the plough which has buried the sweet-scented sward – beneath a sea of barley. In Dorset 20,000 acres of downland in the 1930s was down to only 5,000 in the 1970s. Today, unless they have been acquired as nature reserves, sites survive only where the slopes are too steep to cultivate or they fall within military ranges. These combine in Wiltshire to make it the pre-eminent county for chalk grassland in the kingdom: 70 per cent of what remains of this habitat in England falls within its boundaries. Just under half of Wiltshire's 75,000 acres lie within Ministry of Defence land, while the rest occur on steep valley sides and scarp slopes.

Even in this exceptional county three-quarters of the remaining sites are small and isolated, with areas of less than 50 acres. What was once a continuous carpet has been broken up into a scatter of small mats. Such fragmentation leads to further impoverishment. Surrounded as they are by agricultural land these downland islands are exposed to damage, especially along the margins, from insecticides, herbicides, fertilizers and other modern farm chemicals. This accidental spray-drift leads to the loss of plant and animal species. Furthermore, because they are isolated from other areas of chalk grassland most 'lost' species cannot return by migration across the alien farmland habitat, except in areas where a network of green lanes and protective hedgerows remains. These not only provide highways for humans but act as connecting links along which plants and animals can travel. Their removal impoverishes the landscape and simultaneously adds still further to the problems of conserving one of our most rapidly dwindling wildlife assets.

THE MANGER, NEAR UFFINGTON

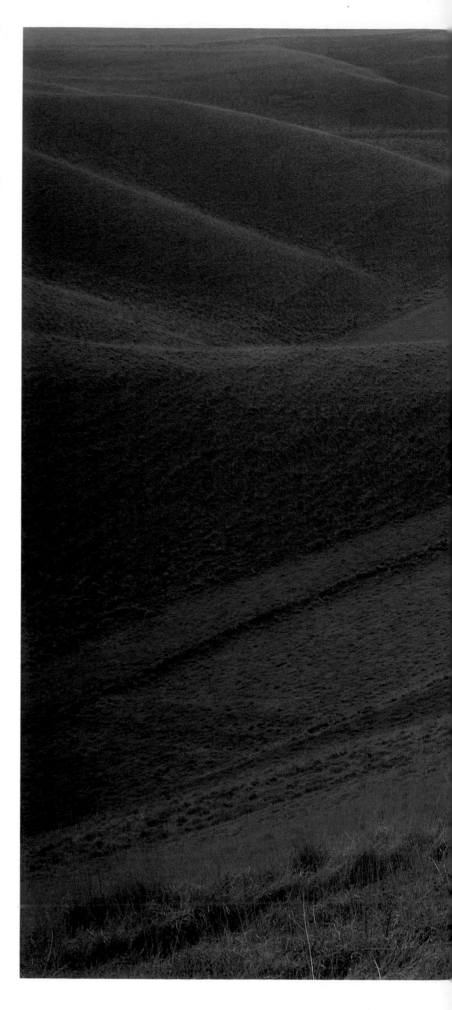

CHICHESTER HARBOUR

RICHARD WILLIAMSON

In August the hot sands of Chichester harbour are drenched twice daily by the tide, rising unnoticed as I wander with bare feet and trousers rolled to the knee. Cool water plunges around the ankles, bubbles of warm air breaking from the sand effervesce between the toes. Feet tired of man-made fibre socks, of rubber soles, of pavements and city streets, rejoice. The mind relaxes. The mind feels strong. It looks at the water's edge, mesmerized by the flattening and smoothing away of other people's footmarks, of the darkening and varnishing of pebbles. It looks along the ribbon of bubbles to where the sea begins. There is a great glassy slide of water out there, a curve going out of sight like the back of a leviathan. That is the power curve of the ocean, bulging and extending, feeling the land of France, of Africa, or the cold far lands of Russia. This is wilderness, which much of our land has lost. One feels it in mountains still. It is drawn from the mountains by the rivers to harbours, estuaries and coastal marshes which are the nerve-endings of a system that connects the mind to distance.

Now it is October. Last sails of the season drift like icebergs. Quietly the harbour empties, exposing tawny sand-bars and shoals of mud. It is not the mud of fighting or misery. It is the mud of life and of light, focused and rearranged light which has already scattered or bounced from clouds or water:

SALTMARSH AT EAST HEAD, CHICHESTER HARBOUR, SUSSEX

the alchemy is astounding. It is a prism, inverting, inventing, blending, bending in blue, or blue-grey, or bluey grey-green.

A few hours later, in darkness, the moon has risen over the muds. The movement of gold water in the channels, of gold curves and black shadows and the sudden glimpse of wildfowl teeming, is as thrilling as the first sight of an Eastern city. Many October nights I have sat on the sea wall till the early hours, watching the sea altering moment by moment as the moon traverses the wintry sky, altering finally to a white glare as the tide floods under the brightest moon of the year. This is *La Mer,* and *Peter Grimes.* Curlews call with their memory of summer on the moors, and this is the *Catalogue d'oiseaux.* All that is best in the world that I have seen and heard is released again. There are three thousand acres of the harbour, enough to make many tons of butter, thousands of gallons of milk, if we rid ourselves of this desire for music.

Do the many people who criss-cross this harbour in their boats hear the music? Do they realize how intricate is the detail that produces this panacea? Or is it to them only a playground? No matter. Their interests do not conflict with the natural world. The money they are prepared to spend on their luxury helps, unbeknown to them, to keep this place as a wilderness. Take away the tide by barrage and the shapes and colours are gone. Industrialize it, and agriculturalize it; allow the many billion animals in the living muds to die by pollution and that mud will become sullen, its gleam lost, as on a dead salmon.

Once I longed to travel in the remote polar regions of Russia, to see the masses of waterfowl, and know that I was on the roof of the world. Now, in winter, with a Russian wind hissing in the marrams, I can be there even so. The harbour is deserted by all those who think of it merely as a playground. The harbour is deserted. But the wildfowl are there in thousands, the wildfowl who keep themselves alive here on their winter holiday from the Arctic wastes. The tide is grey and white, bringing in a scum of grass and reeds. Brent geese rise from nearby fields and spread themselves across the sky in lines, one line above another, rising, falling; a block of black birds, dense as the final pages of a symphony score. The eye strains to follow them, the ear fancies it can hear the boom and grind of ice-floes in their calls. Another connection to distance, which is freedom. Everywhere, on these tidal places, I am reminded of the mass of life on our planet. Shore birds turn and wheel in shoals, like fish in some newly discovered South Sea paradise. Are there five thousand, or ten? Casually they turn and every white belly glances in the sun. Turn again and they are as a smoke plume from a great liner. Again, and they vanish. They weft and warp, unrehearsed but perfect, playing with shapes in the sky. Look at one bird through a powerful glass. A thousand feathers overlap, each different in shape, to waterproof, to glide, to propel, to slide through the air on terrible journeys to Iceland, or Greenland, or Spitsbergen, and back. They are perfect, and this is their place, on these lonely winter waters.

Look at the shoreline after the tide has gone and see the necklace many miles long of sea life formed, lived, and broken up, the ossuary of the oceans; of shells and seaweeds and crustaceans, and eggs of strange creatures as yet undreamed of by most of mankind, altered and renewed daily, to be reformed and used again.

And summer is still to come. The fretting waves of winter will go, and the changing shades of grey will take on colour. I will lie in the sandhills and let slip the grains million by million and feel relaxation in stroking the earth. There will be a buoyant air from the Azores, and azure lines with white froth in the sea and in the air. The air will draw with it the swallows, and the sea swallows, cuckoos and pipits, warblers and hobbies; all will land tiredly among the hills and rest, feed, and fly on into England. Plants will show flowers as small as stars: sea milkwort, stonecrop, sandwort, spurrey; the mind conjures up the names like a huntsman numbering his hounds.

Here I will lie in the sun, where I now crouch against the cold, and touch the hot sand and all its tiny plants and feel the charge of my mother earth. I know that as one of the creatures here, my body moving and being is as amazing as all the others. And as they need this place to live, so do I. I need this contact with the earth, with more than the earth, with the nerves that stretch out from the earth; that stretch through the seas and the skies, that stretch through all that is known of this earth, and that stretch into those

THE ESTUARY, CHICHESTER

SAND DUNES, EAST HEAD

regions that are still unknown. I think we all need this contact, however hard a deal we drive with the devil; perhaps not all the time, perhaps only once a month, or less, perhaps once a year, or perhaps even only once in a lifetime.

It may be that our choice of habitat is formed in childhood – my soul's seedtime was the marshes, and so it is to the marsh that I turn to refresh myself. Sometimes it is enough to see it from a car window, sometimes even just to know it is there. But to know that it had gone, that next summer, and the next winter, I would not be able to come down to this estuary, would not be able to walk over the sands with the wind flattening the skin into my cheeks, would no longer see and hear the wildfowl with their wild, harsh calls, would no longer be able to sit and stare into space – this would be to have that gleam of the mind, or soul, or whatever sacred area we call our own, crushed and replaced with a dreadful dull depression and a will not to live.

MARRAM GRASS IN THE SAND AT EAST HEAD

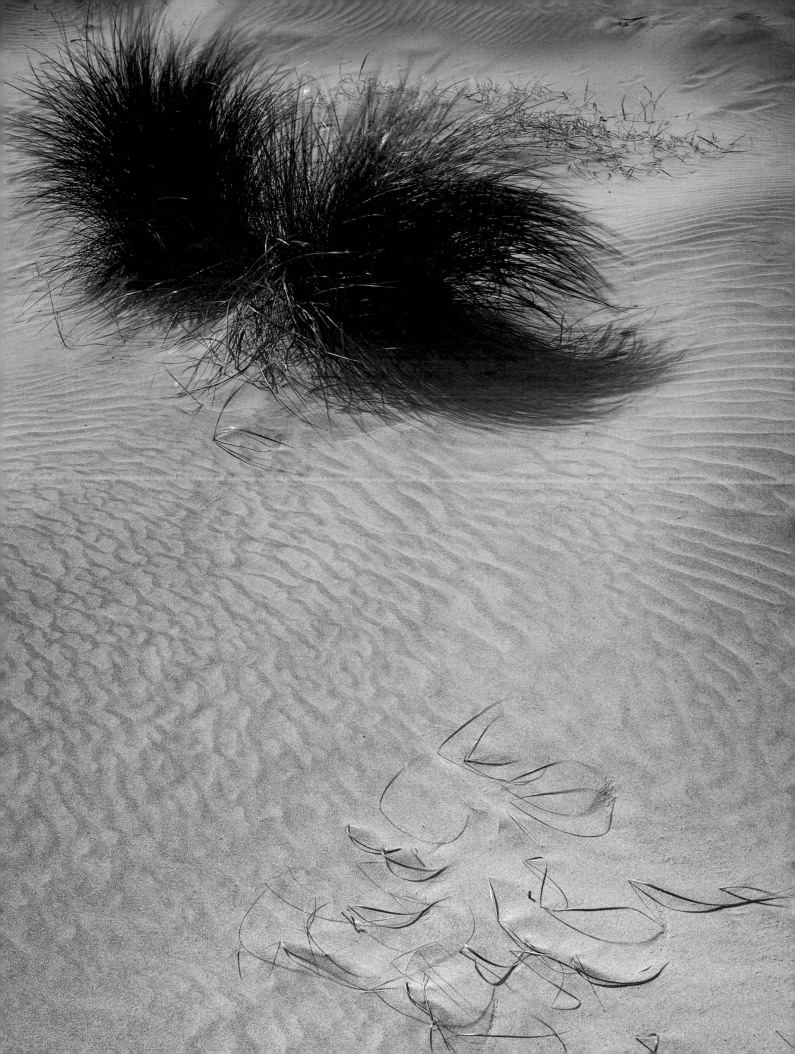

The saltmarshes and mudflats of Britain's estuaries and sheltered bays have long been subject to embankment and reclamation for agriculture. The Romans began the process when they separated the Fens from the Wash, and sea walls around our coast still bear witness to centuries of such enclosure.

The twentieth century has brought its own destructive forces to further diminish this wilderness. Since 1950 the pace of change has quickened. The Nature Conservancy Council has calculated that in thirty years up to 1980 14,000 acres of the 94,000 acres (15 per cent) which existed in 1950 has been reclaimed and in some areas, like the Wash, up to 40 per cent has become farmland. Saltmarshes near large ports have been prime targets for industrial development, and the growth of leisure and the desire to 'muck about in boats' has created a demand for new yacht basins and their associated marina villages. Industry and leisure each produce waste, and thousands more acres near these developments have disappeared under layers of refuse.

Agriculture, industry and leisure have combined in two estuaries to obliterate virtually all the saltmarshes and mudflats they once embraced. At Teesmouth, in the North East, the last 350 acres in an estuary which in 1800 contained 6000 acres is now subject to development, while in Southampton Water, only twenty miles west of Chichester Harbour, most of what little remains has been allocated to industry.

Industry, roads and tips are outward and visible signs of change; with them come less obvious but equally destructive agents in various forms of pollution. Nutrient-enriched domestic and industrial effluents have stimulated the growth of green algae which blanket the mud in summer: this has increased the food supply for geese and wigeon but reduced the area available for some mud-probing waders, thus altering the balance of the bird population. Waders may also be threatened by a build-up of heavy metals in the mud and all estuarine birds near oil terminals and harbours are in constant danger of oil spills.

The almost total loss of the saltmarshes in two of Britain's estuaries should be sufficient warning, but in 1980 29 of our 41 largest intertidal areas were subject to proposals for a different kind of development. One of these proposals presents a new threat which would eclipse in scale any others yet devised for Britain: the Severn Barrage would, if built, have a devastating effect on the saltmarshes upstream, quite apart from the inevitable industrial growth which would follow. And somewhere 'in the air', above either the Severn or the Thames estuary, hangs the shadow of a third London airport which, as planned for Maplin Sands, would engulf over 15,000 acres of estuary now used as wintering grounds by dark-bellied brent geese.

The future of these saltmarshes and mudflats is not the concern of the British alone. We are bound by international agreements to protect wetlands of worldwide ornithological importance. If we allow this erosion to continue we shall lose not only the geese and the waders but our reputation as a nation which cares about its wildlife.

SAND-BARS AT LOW TIDE, CHICHESTER HARBOUR

A SUFFOLK VALLEY WOOD

RONALD BLYTHE

Childhood is, among so much else, a matter of attainable destinations. That early getting about on one's own two feet is a thrilling business. Woods of all shapes and sizes were high up on my desirable destinations list. There were plenty to choose from, although none of them actually spectacular. According to books, woods were where the action was and my heart used to race and thump when I reached them. A few steps into a wood altered all this, switched my expectancy. Its silence, which was really the amalgamated sound of its murmurings and snappings, instantly transformed me from adventurer to contemplative. Except that to prop one's bike against a roadside tree and walk in and in and in needed quite a bit of physical daring as well as that state of mind which, at home, was referred to as 'his mooning'. Serve them right if, poignantly, there were banner headlines shouting, 'LOST BOY'S BICYCLE FOUND AGAINST OAK. WOOD CLAIMS ANOTHER VICTIM'.

When ones comes to think about it, the sole purpose of woods in children's literature is as places to get lost in. It was both a relief and a disappointment to the nine-year-old me to wander half a mile through a Suffolk wood and suddenly step out into a land of non-wood and familiar bearings. Also, it now occurs to me, our local woods were apt to get rather crowded at certain times of the year, bluebell time, blackberry time and just 'wooding' time, when

ELM BARK, ASSINGTON WOOD, SUFFOLK

people of all ages could be seen lugging home the spoils. These were always hauled off in quite immoderate quantities: bluebells in such arm-loads that they slipped steadily for miles, blackberries heaped into fishbags until they soaked through the straw, mutilated fungus (it is strange how so many people are compelled to break a fungus) and a good log which someone couldn't carry another yard. Woods were universal providers of nuts, fruit, fuel, flowers, holly, mistletoe, birds' eggs and so on, and were not then noticeably infested with gamekeepers. Lovers, of course. Woods made girls uneasy and boys brave. 'Going bluebelling' would usually raise a laugh. A gypsy or two might be encamped on the verges. 'My mother said, that I never should/Play with the gypsies in the wood.' Chance would have been a fine thing. They were so exclusive, so unreachable. Their dogs barked but they themselves never said a word.

The wood I liked best was six miles away and was variously referred to as Assington Wood, Assington Thicks, Agar Fen and Tiger Hill, the latter because the tooth of a tiger had been found there. It covered a deep little valley and had a lane running through the middle of it. There was never the least doubt when you reached it that you had come to somewhere very special. A swift, gravelly stream hurried through this ever-fascinating wood on its way to the Stour, and ran bridge-less across the road itself so that everybody had to splash through it. There were also nightingales, 'thick on the ground', as an old woman strangely said, although we knew what she meant.

Almost a lifetime later I find myself within sight of this beloved childhood wood from a house on the south bank of the Stour. Seen from such a distance of time and cornfields, it looks formidable. But when I walk to it, it gradually dissolves from being a dark massif into its old pleasant self. More than ever it constitutes an important destination. It is amazingly unchanged, and because visiting it is less like going back than just going on, I suddenly felt the need to take some kind of stock. It was warm mid-October and a good moment to make an inventory. No nightingales but a yaffle among the diseased elms whose crowns had snapped off, so that they looked like the shelled trees of the Western Front. No blackberries still fit to eat but plenty of sloes and cerise

WOODLAND MOSAIC, ASSINGTON WOOD

OAK AND BUCKLER FERN, ASSINGTON WOOD

spindleberries. Leaves everywhere were thinning but not yet down, and made
their special fleshless autumn sounds, the poplars most of all. There were
token remnants of summer flowers, red campion particularly. Nettles which
only a month ago would have barred the way lay vertical to the earth but were
raising soft, fresh branches from their tumbled old stems, and there was
woody nightshade in abundance. Startling even amongst so much turning
foliage were the intense crimson leaves of the wild cherry, a tree which John
Evelyn called 'mazzards'. The wood was warm, even snug. 'One impulse from
a vernal wood', wrote Wordsworth (had he in mind that profoundly wooded
year at Alfoxden?) could teach one more than 'all the sages can', and the
impulse which Assington generates, if that is the word, is, I now recognize,
intellectual. Here is every grade of existence from soaring bird to mulch. This
is a lightly managed wood which is wayward and a might rough. It is the kind
of woodland which travellers to almost anywhere once had to blunder
through, a thriving mile or two of an earlier England, a woodland like that
painted by Gainsborough in the 1740s at Cornard, which is just up the road.

Assington Wood has always been and continues to be genuine
woodlanders' territory. A few families, hidden from each other but whose
voices sometimes carry through the trees, have lived in it for centuries. Its
modest architecture manages to survive the general dampness and verdour
and remains solid enough. The buildings consist of a little farmhouse with
pointed windows, its tall cart-shed gaping trustingly on to the lane and
crammed with retired implements, and two or three labourers' cottages. The
wood in fact is a tye, or a minute centre of population far from the main
village. It must have bred a distinctive people who lived well on rabbits, birds,
fruit and pure water. Their warrening, draining, lopping pursuits still mark
every foot of the area. It is due to their efforts that Assington offers its
intriguing mixture of total wildness and ancient hand-marks. The small, flinty
fields cultivated all round the wood have now been pulled into one or two vast
fields, still very stony, and the bracken warned off for good. But the occasional
sarsen lies by the field-edge, just as it did long ago. And the wood itself juts in
and out of the corn in such a way that some of the fields are like three-sided

rooms with huge green and brown walls. The adjoining pastures have remained as they were and cap each other in a series of succulent humps, like the cheerful meadows in a child's picture-book. John Nash, who painted all round here, referred to this landscape as the Suffolk–Essex Highlands. These woods never look better than they do in late October, when the penultimate moment of their summer density is scored across this border countryside of new wheat and drillings, sharp distances and vivid skies.

It is usual to be badly let down when one returns to the scenes of youthful excitement, but not so at Assington. These woods do not lure me even one single step towards mind-weakening nostalgia – which is what I expected when I returned to them. I think it is because they have so much going on in them at the moment that they divert one from the past. Even more than the fields – which in any case now seen to have acquired a computerized motion – old, personal-to-one's-self woodlands like Assington–Agar Fen–Tiger Hill possess that powerful cyclic movement which gives a kind of reflective zest to the present. 'Enter these enchanted woods, you who dare,' wrote Meredith in his poem 'The Woods of Westermain', and that is it: the daring to enter what is in effect the jurisdiction of the forest. This modest wood of, perhaps, some fifty acres has always suggested to me a sampling of the forest proper in many of its varieties. It *was* the forest proper when I was a boy. Now it is a sequence of glades, sluices, stands of ash, oak and beech, gardens, flowery banks, scrub, conifers, rabbit runs, tracks – anything a visiting woodlander can ask for.

With the exception of relatively small areas of pine woods in the Highlands of Scotland and yew woods on limestone and chalk in the south and west of Britain, the natural vegetation cover of these islands below the tree line is broad-leaved deciduous woodland. The majority had already been cleared for agriculture by Domesday, and woods only remained where they were of value to the community or too difficult or remote to clear. Almost every parish retained a wood through the Middle Ages, managing it as a source of timber for buildings and for implements, for firewood, fruits and game – a self-sustaining harvest of a wild crop. Larger areas like the New Forest or Rockingham Forest were retained, often by royalty, for fox and deer hunting.

The importance of woodland for the landscape was not fully appreciated until the eighteenth century, whereas a consciousness of its value for wildlife did not emerge until the beginning of this century, by which time half the Domesday woodlands had already been lost to arable and pasture. But no sooner had pioneer conservationists begun to appreciate the variety and wealth of our ancient woodlands than a new threat developed with the establishment of the Forestry Commission in 1919. This body not only planted forests of alien trees in our uplands but also converted lowland woods into plantations of needle-producing, wildlife-blanketing larch, pine and spruce. Beauty, amenity and nature conservation alike were swept aside as maximum timber production became the primary goal. In addition to such direct activities the Commission was able, through a widespread system of grants, to persuade many private landowners to follow suit, a process helped by a variety of tax concessions made available by the Government.

Thus, despite a growing awareness of the importance of our ancient woodlands for their scientific, educational and historical features, their rate of destruction has accelerated. Since 1946, 30-50 per cent of them have been cleared or converted into conifer plantations. If this process continues, we shall over a brief period in the history of our islands have witnessed the conscious vandalism of a part of our national heritage as savage and irresponsible as an intruder cutting all the Turners in the Tate to ribbons or smashing all the medieval glass in York Minster. For once destroyed, these ancient woodlands cannot be re-created: their rich associations of plants and animals, their rare and sensitive species, the local history locked in their banks and ditches, and their thousand-year-old coppiced hazels will have gone for ever. Future generations will rightly point their finger with anger and amazement at an age in which millions had their eyes opened by *Life on Earth* on television while allowing its wonders to be destroyed in the real world beyond their curtained windows.

HONEY FUNGUS, ASSINGTON WOOD

THE FENS

EDWARD STOREY

Today would have been a good day to introduce a stranger to the Fen country: the pale mauve sky of daybreak quickly brightening to a crystalline blue and the landscape coated in that pure light which is a feature of this corner of England.

Light . . . space . . . far distances . . . sky . . . how can one describe this unique and predominately man-made landscape? Some people would, I know, use words such as 'dull', 'flat' and 'colourless'. Not me, especially on such a late spring morning as this. Having spent my life in this kingdom of mists, harvest fields and open country, I know there can be days when the fields look uninvitingly soggy, when the grey clouds sag more like wet sacks and the horizon disappears into a blurred bleakness which can depress. But today the light magnifies and extends all boundaries. This morning the land is shining as if every blade of grass or leaf of new crop is lit from within. Whitewashed farm-buildings twelve miles away stand out with a brilliant clarity as if carved out of snow. Snow would not survive long today, for the air is warm and the dazzle on the land comes from a sun unimpeded by mist or industrial smoke.

You cannot ignore the sun in the Fens. It rises over the eastern ridge of the world in the early morning and continues its regal journey across the great continent of sky, holding court for a moment at the noon's zenith, before its

BURNT FEN, CAMBRIDGESHIRE

WOODWALTON FEN

slow procession to the westerly horizon. There are not many places in Britain where you can witness such a complete arc of the sun's path. It is omnipresent and we are its subjects.

So, yes, we have light, space, distance and sky perhaps unequalled in this country. But there is more. After writing thousands of words on these virtues I still find it difficult to describe adequately the intangible qualities which give my native landscape its special character and appeal. Where then do I begin to justify my claims for it again, or explain the excitement and love I feel for a countryside whose beauties may not be apparent to the casual eye? It is, I admit, an elusive, shy, almost hidden country which is not easy to discover, but it is one worth getting to know a little better.

Do I proceed with these rhapsodic impressions or rely on facts? There must be a little of both. Statistics and historical events in themselves can do no more than present a loom on which to weave a personal interpretation of a country's charm. I have said elsewhere that no part of England can be isolated into a weekend or be judged by a season, least of all the Fen country. A wet sugar-beet season can turn paradise into purgatory. The north-east winds of winter can be pitiless and the frosts will gnaw hungrily into the bones of anyone exposed to those arctic spaces. But in April and May when the oil-seed rape fields are a startling yellow, when the air grows inebriant with the smell of meadowsweet and the acres of barley flow with a silken rustle, there is nowhere to give one a greater sense of pride in man's achievement on the land.

I emphasize man's role in the making of this landscape because it was not always so. There was a time when the Fens rightly earned their name and reputation. Daniel Defoe was not being unkind or inaccurate when he described them as 'the sink for thirteen counties'. Water flowing down from the uplands could not be contained within the winding rivers of the Great Ouse, Nene and Welland. Their banks burst and thousands of acres were constantly under flood. The natural basin formed by the geological eccentricities of time meant that the water, having arrived, could not then flow uphill to the outfalls in the Wash. The problem was often aggravated by

FODDER FEN

the sea walls breaking at high tide so that salt water made its own claims upon the enormous wilderness of marsh and fen. It has taken the ingenuity and vision of man to transform this scene of desolation into the fertile region we can praise today.

This is not the place in which to enlarge on Fen drainage, that fascinating drama of man's struggle with the elements. It is, after all, only part of the history which has gone into the making of the modern Fen country we know today. The Romans, Anglo-Saxons, Scandinavians, Normans and Dutch have also left their influences. Canute, Hereward the Wake, Cornelius Vermuyden and Oliver Cromwell are only some of the characters in the events which have contributed to our story.

As I drove the other day through a world of emerald green fields and saw the solitary figures of men scattered across the land hoeing their sugar-beet crops or harrowing, I knew that I must devote the space on these pages to an impression of what this area has meant to me – why I have spent my writing years exploring the meaning of 'belonging to a place', why I have been content to draw on its ancient springs for most of that writing. It is a land I have known since I was born in the Isle of Ely more than fifty years ago, a land in which I grew up surrounded, not only by the vast Cambridgeshire Fens, but also by the people who worked on the land. In those far off days I took that world of limitless space and extravagant skies for granted. I did not question why the land was so flat, the soil so black, the countryside so sparse of trees, the rivers so important. I imagined that the rest of the world was the same. I knew nothing of mountains, lakes, valleys or woodlands. My world was as flat and green as a billiard table. It belonged in essence to the wind and skylarks, herons and reed-mace. It was a world of newly ploughed furrows and wheatfields, of long, grass-bordered roads embroidered with dandelions, toad-flax, poppies, vetch and wild iris. Not for twenty years did I realize that the Fens were different, and it was even longer before I appreciated the importance of the relationship which is slowly established between a man and his landscape.

But is the 'spirit of place', I began to wonder, something we create for our

REEDS AND WILLOW, WOODWALTON FEN

own needs, projecting our feelings into the landscape, making *it* accept us rather than *we* accept it? Or does the landscape itself have a spirit which we learn to recognize, absorb, interpret and draw from until, in the end, we are unmistakaby shaped or conditioned by the very nature of the soil from which we come?

I found the answer in Laurens van der Post's book *Jung and the Story of Our Time,* in which he recalls how the great thinker told him repeatedly that 'the nature of the earth itself has a profound influence on the character of the people born and raised on it . . . ' Jung could not offer any scientific proof that this was so but, from his lifetime's study of people, he maintained that a character became an expression of the soil.

Many of the characters I have known and written about were to confirm this view for me, and I began to feel that I was part of a long (and largely unwritten) tradition. The people I knew were undoubtedly 'expressions of the soil', especially those who had lived and worked in the Fens for most of their lives. They had that far-distant look in their eyes, that quiet but belligerent response to life that has known all the vicissitudes of nature – the cruel winters and the beneficent summers, the winds, floods, seasons and harvests which they have learned how to conquer and control, creating this landscape which we can now enjoy. Whether they work with animals or machines, they are the living evidence of Jung's belief. They are an integral part of the land just as the land is part of them. Their behaviour and their attitudes are conditioned by it and, one hopes, always will be.

Since I began writing about the Fens much has, inevitably, changed – sometimes for the better, sometimes not. Not only is the rich peatland (formed over thousands of years from an age when the Fens were as wooded as anywhere in England) shrinking to a disturbing level, but the demands of society today are also diminishing that land. Fields which were a feature of the landscape just ten years ago have now surrendered to the bulldozers and developers. Quiet lanes have become busy roads and minor roads have become dual carriage-ways. Farm machinery now costs four or five times what it did and the value of land has reached prices which, for our grandparents, would have bought half the country. East Anglia has become a fashionable place in which to live, and old-established communities are losing something of their traditional identity. But I can still reflect on the virtues of this land and find my feelings for it unchanged, my loyalties unaltered by time, my roots unsevered. Where else, I ask again, could I find this clarity of light and expanse of space to thrill the spirit as well as the eye? Where else could I feel so at home with the unending rituals of man and the soil, or be so at ease with an awareness of the past as well as the present?

Whether I travel between those 'once-upon-a-time' islands on which the great Fenland abbeys were built, or sit by rivers that have been tamed and straightened by modern engineers, I am conscious of being part of a daily pattern which has made sense not only of a place but of life itself. Would that stranger I spoke of at the beginning understand me a little better now or have a deeper appreciation of what this country means to me? I hope so.

> Today I met a man who shares
> My fascination with these fields.
> He said 'It is not what you see,
> It's what you know. Each furrow
> Is a lifeline on the hand. Each reed
> A symbol of our ancestry.' I stand
> And in the silence hear again
> Familiar voices rising from the ground.

I need no more than that assurance, no more than a day like this to remind me of who I am. Light . . . space . . . far distances . . . sky . . . and voices rising from the ground.

Every year, as a result of government-subsidized agricultural drainage and improvement schemes, up to 150,000 acres of wetlands in Britain are destroyed. Marshes and water meadows have disappeared at such a rate that in many lowland English counties only a handful now remain, and only those which are nature reserves are safe. Ironically the largest and most important of these runs through the heart of the Fens, from Earith to Denver, and is an artefact of their drainage by man.

The Ouse Washes is an area of 6000 acres of square fields and ditches lying between the straight cuts of the Old and New Bedford Rivers which are part of a scheme begun by Cornelius Vermuyden in the seventeenth century: over two-fifths is now owned and managed by the Wildfowl Trust, the Royal Society for the Protection of Birds and the Cambridgeshire Naturalists' Trust. The area acts as a temporary reservoir for flood water when the river Ouse is carrying more than can pass out to sea. This shallow 'lake' with its varying depths of water attracts up to 60,000 wildfowl in winter, teal, wigeon, pintail, mallard, shoveler and pochard being the most numerous. But of all the visitor the most important are the swans – not the resident black-billed mute swans but Bewick's and whoopers which breed in Scandinavia and north Russia and pass the winter in north-west Europe. The 2300 or so Bewick's which come to the Ouse Washes represent about 20 per cent of the world population of this handsome yellow-billed species.

The assembly of so many birds has for long attracted wildfowlers. In the past the majority were responsible members of Wildfowl Clubs who shot relatively small numbers of unprotected species, retrieved them with trained dogs, and learned more about ducks and swans during their long, cold vigils than most professed naturalists.

In the last ten years, however, the standard of shooting has fallen as the number of guns has increased. Many birds are shot at beyond killing range, and are thus 'pricked' which enables them to fly beyond the recovery range of the shooter, who rarely has a dog, so the birds die slowly and painfully. Totally protected species such as the Bewick's swan are also shot at: X-rays of captured birds show that 34 per cent of them carry lead pellets.

Another consequence of the growth of wildfowling has been the build-up of spent lead shot. The pellets move very slowly down through the soil and are thus likely to be picked up by wildfowl, a considerable number of which die each year from lead poisoning.

The problems are not unique to the Ouse Washes: they stem from a system which allows anyone with a gun to buy a day-ticket to shoot at wildfowl on private land. These 'cowboys', through ignorance or indifference, often fire at anything with feathers – even lapwings and skylarks are frequently killed. The only remedy is to institute a shooting test which must be passed by all those wishing to shoot wildfowl: it would include bird recognition and the law. In addition, shooting without dogs should not be allowed and steel shot should be obligatory in areas of heavy shooting to reduce the risks of lead poisoning.

THE WASH AND HUNDRED FOOT DRAIN

THE BLACK MOUNTAINS

JAN MORRIS

Some mountain ranges seem to have burst out of the earth's surface in exuberant explosion, taking the snow for their summits with them. Not Mynydd Du, the Black Mountains of south-eastern Wales, which lie in a brooding clump beside the English border, where Gwent, Powys and Herefordshire meet. They appear to have heaved themselves from the subterrain with infinite grave toil, and so they stand there with a sullen sort of beauty, geologically spent.

They are instantly recognizable. Whether you approach them out of England or out of deeper Wales, their long hunched silhouette stands like a rampart before you, apparently impenetrable – and if you should happen to approach them out of space, satellite photographs demonstrate, they show as a hefty blodge of brown like no other in sight. They are the most cohesive of the mountain massifs of Wales: ten miles long at their longest point, two and a half thousand feet at their loftiest cairn, never more than eight miles across, roughly oblong in shape and intersected only by three narrow valleys, two of them dead ends, in which perhaps five hundred people live. There are four churches hidden among them, four chapels, three pubs: there are several hundred ponies and what appear to be a couple of million sheep.

They are said to be called the Black Mountains because a combination of

WAUN FACH FROM DARREN LWYD, POWYS

THE BLACK MOUNTAINS FROM MYNYDD EPPYNT, POWYS

situation, light and foliage really does give them a sable look, shadowed with dark patches even in the sunshine: but they are metaphysically sombre too, full of wistful nuance. They are rather sad mountains: wonderfully beautiful, lyrical in some moods, sheep-speckled and wind-whistled, but sad.

There is something hallucinatory to their presence. Bracken covers most of the range, conifers lap the lower slopes, and those long twisting valleys, each with its fast-flowing stream, are sunk deep in the moorland. The air is utterly pure, except for mist, the light is pellucid, except when it drizzles, but something about the ordering of the whole, some particular refraction of atmosphere perhaps, makes scale and substance all illusory.

Take Mr Jones's farm – there, just to the left of the coppice, a small grey sprawl of stone, a barn with an iron roof, a tumble of tractors and half-dismantled cars, and Mr Jones himself, with his dogs, gathering the sheep in the field above (staccato shouts on the wind across the valley, chirp of whistle, scud of white woolly shapes across the meadow to the gate). He is not very far away, only half a mile or so, but he and his animals seem infinitely remote or reduced, all in crystal miniature. It is like looking through the wrong end of a telescope: some prism of the place puts not just Mr Jones, but all man's little works, permanently at a distance.

I sometimes think the church of the martyred St Isio, in the central valley of the three, is an illusion of an extremer kind, for if at one moment I can see it clear as daylight from my garden, at the next it seems to have vanished altogether. Is it really there at all? Often it seems no more than a dapple in the woods: and even when I have walked there, to make a wish at its holy well perhaps, or wonder once more at the red ochre skeleton upon the wall (painted so the local lore maintains in human blood) – once I have shut the churchyard gate behind me again, the trees close in once more and the light shifts, it is as though I have just imagined church, well, skeleton, martyred St Isio and all.

The web of time is looser here than in most places, too, and images tend to overlap. In a year or two cottages rebuilt as weekend retreats by Reading

GRWYNE FAWR, MYNYDD DU FOREST, POWYS

SPHAGNUM BOG, PENTWYNGLAS, POWYS

sociology lecturers, with Habitat bunks and Japanese paper lanterns, tend to look as utterly indigenous as the most shambled of the valley farms: and when the trekkers are out, and you see the long line of their ponies trailing across the flank of a hill, or tethered in the yard of the Rising Sun, they might just as well be the beasts of pack-horse men or medieval cavalry.

Even the fabric of the hills can be deceptive. Those gloomy stains on the moorland may resolve themselves, as you get nearer, into marvellous purple expanses of heather and bilberry: sometimes even the spare exhaustion of the Black Mountains turns out to have life and vigour after all, young horses are playing about up there on the ridges, grouse start in panic as you pass, and high above Disgwylfa, the Watching Place, skylarks sing in ecstasy.

Almost like tunnels the valleys thread their way into these hills, and they seem to invite secrets. For a few years in the 1920s a little steam train ran up and down the valley of the Grwyne Fawr, taking workers and materials to the reservoir at the top, but now no public transport reaches the Black Mountains. With their wild but compact intensity of form, so aloof to the pastoral country outside, they are like a refuge: you feel they could be locked off, with great steel gates at each valley mouth, for the containment of reclusives.

It was here they say that Dewi Sant, Saint David, set up his first hermitage beside the Honddu River, living on the wild leeks that were to become the symbol of his nation. Here the Augustinians came, in their search for the ideal solitude, to build the magnificent priory of Llanthony whose grey walls still stand there jagged and frondy – there is an inn in the old Abbot's house, and you may take your Real Ale, with a hamburger and chips, into the roofless ruin. Here too came, in the 1880s, the visionary Father Ignatius, to pursue convictions no less vivid, to see in fact the Virgin herself in a holly bush at Capel-y-Ffin, to establish his own community and to lie now, still visited by pilgrims, in his grave in the nave of its ruined chapel.

There is an air of sweet retreat to the little square church of Capel-y-Ffin, near the top of the Honddu valley, which Francis Kilvert the diarist likened to

MAT-GRASS ON PEN TRUMAU, POWYS

HAY BLUFF, OFFA'S DYKE, POWYS

86   AFON HONDDU, GWENT

an owl. There is a suggestion of raffish collusion to the derelict house of the Hermitage, at the top of the Grwyne Fach, in which we are told long ago a local swell maintained his mistresses. There is a disturbingly enigmatic power to the church of St Martin at Cwmyoy, which has been knocked all skew-whiff by subsidence or landslide, and stands there on its hillside altogether out of true, nothing perpendicular, nothing right-angled, nothing self-explanatory.

And about the scattered inhabitants of the hills, in the two hamlets of the Honddu, in the isolated farms and villages elsewhere, there is an unmistakable sense of withdrawal. Some of course are not true inhabitants at all, only weekend recreationists from England, but others have been here since the beginning of time, and seem enfolded in their mountains. Dark and hidden things still happen among them – incest, suicide, mental breakdowns, irreconcilable feuds over wills or boundaries – and the faces of the farmers are often set in a resentful mould, as though they suspect you of leaving a gate open: a gate not simply of their yard or sheep-pen, but of their sensibilities.

Prehistoric earthworks, east and west, guard the entrances to the Black Mountains, for if these hills have something of the quality of a haven, or a ghetto perhaps, they are also a natural fortress. They stand in country which was disputed for centuries by Welsh and English, and even now they are a kind of no-man's-land between cultures. When the Normans seized the rich Gwent lowlands in the twelfth century, the Welsh were mostly banished to higher, less productive, less accessible country: and nowhere was more proper for natives than the brackeny massif of the Mynydd Du, its valleys choked then with impenetrable forests of beech and oak.

Standing on several kinds of frontier – between countries, between counties, between languages, between dioceses, between languages – the Black Mountains have always been just the place for outlaws and recusants, and even now you might say that the central point of the whole range, the pivot around which its character and meaning revolves, is the old standing stone called Carreg Dial, the Stone of Revenge, which supposedly commemorates the one historic tragedy of these hills. Here in the year 1135 the Norman Earl of Clare, travelling to Talgarth from Y Fenni, Abergavenny, was ambushed by a commando of Welsh guerrillas, led by Morgan ap Owen of Caerleon. The Norman and his retainers were killed, every one, down to the very minstrel, in the dark woodlands which still stand thick above the Grwyne Fawr, and those susceptible to such things still feel a chill *frisson* when they pass that way, and fancy hatreds there.

Lovely though it looks to weekend visitors, in the hush of its remoteness, this has seldom been an innocent kind of country. According to Walter Savage Landor, who had property here in the 1800s, its people were then said to be the most lawless in Britain, and vagabond habits linger. Geese tend to be stolen shortly before Christmas; sheep are rustled; black-leather troops of motor cyclists sweep shatteringly through woodlands on bank holidays; rumours flit about, of fugitives hiding in upland barns, of criminals storing explosives, or distilling drugs, or making blue movies, in their dainty weekend cottages. The mountains welcome as their own the humped forms of the soldiers, their faces blackened, their guns slung, so often to be seen disappearing up the stony tracks, like Morgan ap Owen and his toughs before them, to rehearse their brutal craft.

Visitors from England, tramping the ridge-tracks of the Black Mountains, find the strange stillness of the place a consolation. Visitors out of Welsh Wales are more likely to find in it a haunting suggestion of abandonment. For though these mountains are in Wales, and offer landscapes as absolutely Welsh as you could find, long ago the living Welshness left them, and retreated further west, over beyond Brecon and Builth, into the hinterland. Hardly a soul speaks the Welsh language now: even Welsh radio and television, rebuffed by the high escarpment, does not reach these valleys.

But to a Welsh imagination there are echoes everywhere of the old lost culture, its style and its vocabulary. Up on the mountain I often imagine I hear the Welsh songs and banter of the cattle-drovers who used to pass this way out of the interior, stopping at inns that are now no more than piles of rubble, pounding their beasts in enclosures that are only unexpected patches of green among the bracken. It is easy to suppose those grey farms down there still with a harp in the parlour, and a poet at his books, and all too easy to think for a moment, when a distant voice sounds across the valley, that it is a cry in the old language – so all-but-Welsh does the dialect still sound, so close in intonation, if not in actual words, to that magnificent original!

Immediately to the south of the Black Mountains there stands a solitary outlier, Pen-y-Fal, the Sugar Loaf. This splendid peak is the very antithesis of the mountains themselves. It really does seem to have sprouted from the earth in an instant flowering of sandstone confidence, and it stands there grandly conical and commanding, looking southward, eastward, outward, anywhere but northward into the melancholy massif. On a breezy day of sunshine it is a fine thing to climb its summit and look down upon the rich vales of Gwent and Glamorgan, away to the shining strip of the Bristol Channel and easy green Somerset beyond.

For myself, though, I never face that way for long. Something always makes me turn, back towards the old bare hulk of Mynydd Du. Some nagging magnetism of those mountains compels me: as though there is unfinished, unspecified business awaiting me there, out of my own and my people's past.

Until the Second World War the gorse and heather covered hills of western Britain were a vivid contrast to the measured arable and grassland fields of the lowlands. Many of the plants and animals which had once been common everywhere, but were lost through drainage and cultivation in the lowlands, still survived in boggy valleys and unimproved moorlands, and there was a part of our islands where one could climb out of a human-infested, agrico-industrial landscape into a flowery wilderness disturbed only by the croak of ravens and the cry of curlew. In the last forty years that wilderness had been consistently eroded – for nothing.

During the war the need for this country to be self-sufficient in food was obvious. When the war ended, despite increasing opportunities to shop elsewhere, the theory persisted that we must maximize production, even from our marginal hill-lands where farming could never be profitable unless supported by huge subsidies.

So, over the years, successive governments have poured taxpayers' money into the hills to pay farmers to increase yields. Grants of 70 per cent have been available for field drainage and of 50 per cent to convert moorland rich in wildflowers to monotonous green pastures. To these have been added headage payments: for every cow kept the rate is currently £35, for every sheep £5.50. In all, 75 per cent of the income of hill farmers has come from grants to produce food which could have been bought more cheaply elsewhere, in the process destroying a wildlife heritage which can never be replaced.

The absurdity of this policy has become even more apparent since Britain joined the EEC and we found ourselves in a community producing surpluses. Even the relatively small amounts our hill-lands do create (about one-twelfth of the total output from 25 per cent of the land) contribute to butter-mountains and milk-lakes which, under Common Market rules, have to be bought at a guaranteed price, stored in expensive warehouses, and later sold at give-away prices.

This farce cannot be allowed to continue. Government must surely recognize that subsidies limited to the narrow objective of producing food we do not want must end, and that ways must be found to preserve the wilderness so that those who visit it may enjoy its peace and inspiration. Subsidies should be used instead to encourage farmers to play a part in protecting the beauty of the land they live on and conserving its wildlife. Funding must be channelled into rebuilding stone walls, improving footpaths, managing heather moors by traditional burning, maintaining unpolluted ponds and streams, and planting copses for firewood and nesting birds. By these means the same amount of money which is now spent on destroying the uplands could be used to retain the wilderness for our enjoyment and to give wildlife another chance, while at the same time providing the farmer with a satisfying life and a decent livelihood.

THE VALE OF EWYAS, GWENT

A THICKET IN LLEYN

R.S. THOMAS

Leave it for me: a place in Lleyn, where I may repair to mend my feelings. Woods are scarce in Pen Llŷn, trees even. And this is only a thicket, but dear: 'Infinite riches in a little room.' It is, where I hide, where only the light finds me, filtering through the leaves in summer, and in winter the flash from a blade brandished by the sea nearby.

I watch the farm girl go by, unaware of me, and murmur to myself:

> *Blodau'r flwyddyn yw fy anwylyd,*
> *Ebrill, Mai, Mehefin hefyd,*
> *Llewyrch haul yn tywynnu ar gysgod*
> *A gwenithen y genethod.*

> (My love is all the months of the year,
> April, May, June too;
> the sun's light in a dark place,
> the wheat-germ among the girls.)

I approach it warily. It is nervous. Pfft! A sparrow-hawk is plucked from a branch, like an arrow from a bow. A magpie scolds, out of sight. The place sighs and is still. I wait, and tune my breath to its own. Is it autumn? A dead

NEAR NANHORON, GWYNEDD

MALE-FERN AND GOLDEN SAXIFRAGE, NEAR TAN-Y-GRAIG

leaf stirs and shows its red breast. Is it spring? There is a trickle of song from the bare twigs, where the first willow-warbler is newly arrived among the catkins, its throat also a catkin. In the small pool about the roots of the trees there is a movement, as frogs surface to regard me without change of expression on their primeval faces. So little by little the life of the thicket is resumed and I am forgotten. The dragon-fly quivers its wings in the light's rainbow, before bulleting off into the shade. A bird snaps its bill on an ephemeral insect. A luckier beetle runs unmolested up a tree's bark.

This is a thoroughfare for migrants, warblers in spring, thrushes in autumn. Once on a day in October, after the gales had stripped it, it was alive with goldcrests. The air purred with their small wings. To look up was to see the twigs re-leafed with their bodies. Everywhere their needle-sharp cries stitched at the silence. Was I invisible? Their seed-bright eyes regarded me from three feet off. Had I put forth an arm, they might have perched on it. I became a tree, part of that bare spinney where silently the light was splintered, and for a timeless moment the birds thronged me, filigreeing me with shadow, moving to an immemorial rhythm on their way south.

Then suddenly they were gone, leaving other realities to return: the rustle of the making tide, the tick of the moisture, the blinking of the pool's eye as the air flicked it; and lastly myself. Where had I been? Who was I? What did it all mean? While it was happening, I was not. Now that the birds had gone, here I was once again. Such things, no doubt, had occurred before and other humans had been present, had been a part of them for their own timeless moment, before returning to themselves, involuntary prodigals. Was this Coleridge's experience? To him, you remember, it was the imagination which was primary: 'a repetition in the finite mind of the infinite I AM.' Is that what had happened to me? Had that infinite I announced itself in a thicket in Lleyn, in the serenity of the autumnal sunlight, in the small birds that had taken possession of it, and in the reflection of this in a human being? And had the I in me joined seemingly unconsciously in that announcement; and is that what eternity is? And was the mind that returned to itself but finite mind?

There was something missing from all this. It was too like talk of the

SALLOW IN FLOWER NEAR NANHORON

AFON DWYFACH

MALE-FERN AND HART'S-TONGUE, NEAR NANHORON

PRIMROSES, GLYN-DWYFACH

minute drop returning to the boundless ocean. Such an interpretation smacked too much of the endlessly repeated life-cycle. 'That out of life's own self-delight had sprung the abounding, glittering jet', sang Yeats, memorably but how truthfully? Life is not I; is certainly not God. There is a conventional magnifying of life at the expense of the I. But what is that? Life feeds on life, and has an unconscious, inscrutable, repetitive quality. What talons and beaks were not in waiting for the goldcrests on their way south, to be themselves devoured later by the huge maw of the sea over which other goldcrests would return north on the spring passage?

No, while the experience lasted, I was absent or in abeyance. It was when I returned to myself that I realized that I was other, more than the experience, able to stand back and comprehend it by means of the imagination, and so by this act of creation to recognize myself not as lived by, but as part of the infinite I AM.

Lleyn is a peninsula, battered by wind and sea. There are a few small woods and thickets. Some of them even have names, Welsh names. I am not telling you where this one is, lest too many go there to deflower it. But leave it and others like it for the individual to have such experiences in. Maybe it is only a minute strand of the great web of being, but once broken it cannot be repaired. So with all the means available today do not uproot it or level it in an act of misplaced tidiness or improved farming. I see it as ribs of a body; body as the incarnation of spirit, and spirit returns to eternity and significance when it declares: I am, holding all things in balance; spiralling outward upon itself into infinite space and inward towards the smallest of atoms, awake or dormant in a thicket in Lleyn.

Hazel thickets and copses in the west of Britain often mark the site of ancient oakwoods long since felled, but within their shade they still shelter the relics of native woodland plant and animal communities which have survived on that very spot for several millenniums.

Hazel in a hedge is almost always an indication of its ancient origin, derived perhaps from adjacent woodland, now replaced by arable or pasture, but still accompanied by other woodland shrubs like holly, spindle and field maple and harbouring at their base woodland flowers such as bluebell, dog's mercury or wood anemone.

A landscape of knots of copse and strings of hedges provides a network of pathways along which woodland plants may spread and woodland animals can run and shelter. The widespread felling of copses and uprooting of hedges has not only disastrously damaged the landscape of Britain but has destroyed most of the wildlife which once enriched the sights and sounds of the countryside, leaving only small islands in a sea of arable or featureless grassland.

This process has been slower in the west of England, where copses and hedges are still valued by the livestock farmer as shelter for his sheep and cattle, and well-maintained hedges act as living stock-proof fences. In the east, however, where arable farms prevail and these features no longer have any farming function, thousands of acres of copses and tens of thousand miles of hedges have been grubbed up. Nevertheless in some areas a landscape of copses and hedges does remain, almost entirely due to the shooting or foxhunting interests of the owner or tenant. Copses provide cover and shelter for foxes, while a well-kept hedge makes an excellent jump. There is little doubt that if the anti-foxhunting lobby were successful many more copses and hedges would disappear and the interests of wildlife conservation would be further damaged.

Hedges are important for game preservation, especially where they have been laid to form a base of almost prostrate live branches through which new growth springs up. This produces a thick bottom which is an excellent nesting place for pheasants and partridges, while the plants and insects they harbour are a prolific source of food for adults and their chicks. Hedges also provide shelter for marksmen, hiding the guns from the birds and causing low-flying partridges in particular to rise into a position where they can be shot.

Although many people may be offended by this slaughter in our countryside, it must be remembered that most of the birds killed have been raised artificially and that the benefits to wildlife can be substantial, especially if the hedges are sympathetically managed. Ideally the hedges should be laid periodically and kept trimmed to heights of between four and seven feet, with work concentrated into late winter after all the berries have been eaten by the birds but before the nesting season begins.

If we want to retain in Britain a traditional landscape of copses and hedges in arable areas it may be necessary to find ways of paying farmers to maintain these features. A redistribution of grants to those farmers who recognize their importance to the landscape and wildlife is long overdue.

HAZEL AND RAMSONS, NEAR BODFUAN

THE LAKES

MELVYN BRAGG

'The prospect changes', wrote Thomas Gray, 'every ten paces.' He was writing, in the eighteenth century, of a walk into Borrowdale, but for me, as for many who know the Lakes, his sentence could be the district's epigraph. The prospect – and not only the view – changes continuously.

I was brought up a few miles to the north of it, and yet from the Lake District I drew the single most dominating feature in the landscape of my childhood: Skiddaw. An ancient broad slack-pelted fell, it beckoned and brooded on the southern horizon and we must have looked at it a dozen times a day, for the weather, out of habit and possibly for luck. To me as a child 'The Lakes' were indeed a magic place, rarely visited but on those special occasions full of wonders – great boulders which stood poised to hurtle down cliff-sides, waterfalls that dropped sheer down glistening slate, and the Lakes themselves, oceans of imagination to us, then, as we swished across them on Edwardian pleasure boats. I would have believed without too much pause that Excalibur did indeed rise out of Bassenthwaite Lake from where Tennyson was inspired to conjure it.

Adolescence admitted me to the Youth Hostel Association and walking the length and breadth of the place. Hot summer slogs up Scafell, hours lost in mist on top of Hardknott, calm courting evenings in Patterdale, saturated days

SCAFELL PIKES FROM HARD KNOTT, CUMBRIA

in the Eastern Fells looking for a hostel that seemed to have disappeared back into the hills like the fabled Arthurian rocks in St John's. I went to university thinking I knew the district and feeling sophisticated because I had decided that Wordsworth was good.

During the next ten years I visited the Lakes only now and then but always, truly, felt almost winded with pleasure at the sight and smell of them. Instant waves of resolution – to find a local cottage, to find a local job – broke on the dread rocks of mortgage, ambition and the perilous gathering of metropolitan pleasures. But the place came south with me and figured more and more in my fiction, though, perhaps unsurprisingly since the novels I write aspire to authenticity, the action hovered about the edges of the Lakes. Only occasionally did the fiction penetrate into the massif central which is the rock core. Founded as it was on an early stratum of recollected imagination, it held true to that and circled the border. Even when I eventually bought a small cottage it was in the northernmost tip of the National Park; just in it by less than half a mile.

Once settled into a routine of regular visits, I began to discover the place a second time. Partly through books: W. G. Collingwood, Norman Nicholson, William Rollinson, and further back into the eighteenth century West, Hutchinson, Gilpin, besides the Wordsworths, Coleridge, de Quincy, Southey, Harriet Martineau, Ruskin, Canon Rawnsley – the Lake District must have provided as much literature as any comparable area in Europe. The chief discoveries, though, came from my own walking and from my desire to learn about the place, to sit down and find out about its geology, its history, its industries, legends and traditions. What I unearthed was the foundation which supported and reinforced my previous passionate response: that the Lake District is demonstrably extraordinary. That upsweep of exalted feelings is raised on layers of material contributions which have deeply sprung the place.

It is a geologist's Valhalla. In Rhoughton Ghyll, for instance, where the big belly of a Northern Fell has been slit open for the operation of mining, twenty-three different minerals can be found within a few score yards;

including silver. These fells were laid down about 600 million years ago, and their undeniable similarity to massive docile elephants gently round-backed asleep ought not to lull any climber or walker into an easy feeling of superiority: the Northern Fells claim victims year in, year out. Further south, in the volcanics of the Ordovician period, even more fatal accidents occur; where once volcanic ash spurted and lava poured, bare and jagged rock now provides the testing ground for the Hard Men with their ropes and jangling ironware. Just a few miles south again, yet another geological age accreted its foundation 350 million years ago; then there were times of desert, followed by great bucklings, until finally the ice came and carved the district into its present contour. The result of this multiple activity within a very small space is what observers over the last two centuries have described as a unique and intriguingly varied landscape. Climb any fellside and, as the elegiac Gray truly said, the prospect indeed changes every ten paces. The rombustuous weather, hurtling across the Atlantic, sweeping over Ireland and the Irish Sea to be tossed up by the hills, adds varying colour and swiftly altered skies to the slowly changing earthscape. Nothing is regular, nothing is symmetrical, nothing is still. The earth movements go on, and it is as if the apparent antique settlement of the land is being constantly undermined by a subterranean restlessness — like coral reefs of minerals — which matches the often violent variability of the skies.

After the ice, the landscape was man-made. Over the years the greatest change has been the cutting of the forests; begun about 5000 BC by Neolithic man with his stone axe, the 'progress' of man in this district has been vitally linked to the destruction of trees. Even so, in the Middle Ages the greatest forest in the land was here, and the slaughter of 400 deer in a day by the King and his courtiers was not an uncommon event. But the Germans who came to open up the copper and lead mines at the end of the sixteenth century used so much wood that they were forced to dig for coal. Wars, charcoal burners and the steady demand for domestic fuel did the rest. The Fells are bare. Their nakedness is now emphasized — or is it embarrassed? — by the odd little fig leaf of reafforested conifers. The pelt smoothness has a rock-hard grandeur which

WASTWATER

THIRLMERE

ANGLETARN PIKES FROM ANGLE TARN

is deeply attractive to many of those who regularly come here. To them the mineral-speckled rock cropping out of the bracken, the bare hillsides which crest and furl like great frozen waves, the ingenious rivulations of the valleys unimpeded by deciduous bushiness are the characteristics that they most love about the place.

Like anywhere else, though perhaps here more evident, there are layers of settlement which make the landscape the open air textbook of a lengthy historical adventure. The most picaresque remains are the mysterious stone circles – notably at Castlerigg and Salkeld – still undecoded; there are Iron Age settlements high on the Fells, a reminder, among other things, that once this place was warmer and calmer; Roman remains – one spectacular 'enchanted fortress in the air' sitting side-saddle high on Hardknott Pass; the great Bewcastle and Gosforth crosses; Norman abbeys (most striking is Furness Abbey in Barrow, its sandstone glowing in the sunset); castles ringing the central mountains, guarding exits and entrances but by their very distance from the heart of the place lending credibility to the notion that the heart of the place was never conquered by the French – just as it was merely occupied, never crushed by the Romans. The sweep of building continued until its peak in the sixteenth and seventeenth centuries which brought to the district those enviable, secure, stone-built farm houses which seem planted on the hillsides or as inevitable in a valley bottom as the river bed itself. And finally the gentrification, happily in local materials: the subtly coloured grey and blue slates of Honister, Kirkby and Tilberthwaite and the Victorian baronial gothic clustered mainly around Bowness-on-Windermere are by no means an unpleasant addition. In short, then, as you walk the Fells – and it is as if the district had been designed for walking – you can rely on being enlivened by contact with the different intrusions of man. For just as it can still be a lonely place, so it has on that surface which is so dominating, enough well-defined and, generally, well-executed traces of previous encounters between men and the landscape to be a constant refreshment.

The heart of the Lakes is the hill farms, and it is the hill farmers, for me, who carry the real life of the district. Without them the land itself would soon

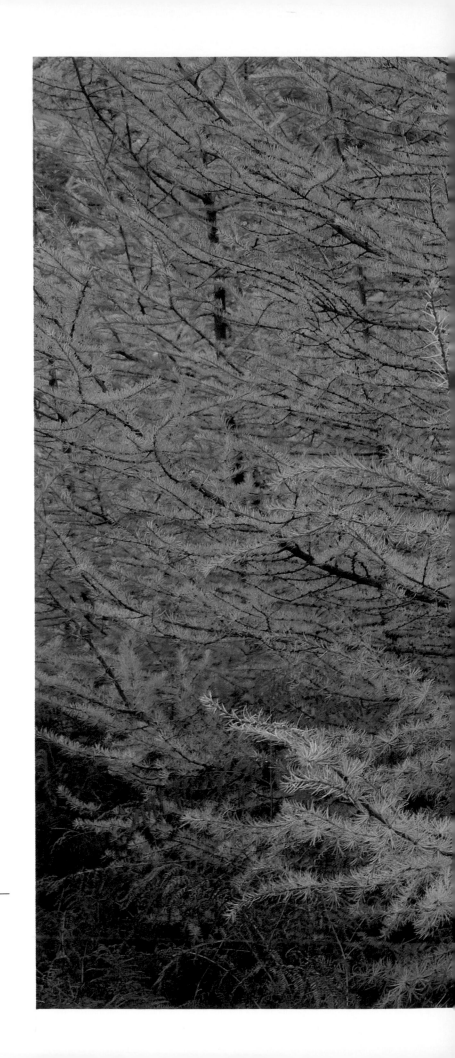

AUTUMN LARCHES, SMAITHWAITE BANKS

fatten and sprawl into unkempt parkland; without them the area would become no more than a natural playground. That it is still a place of work – and tough work – strengthens it profoundly: gives it that basic, functioning reality without which ski resorts and the like can seem to be mere toy-towns. The farmers maintain the dialect – almost wholly Norse and still miraculously surviving after nine centuries of opposition; they sustain the local sports – fell running, wrestling, hound trailing, foot hunting. It could be argued, romantically but with some supporting evidence, that deep in the heart of the district are still the descendants of those Brigantes unquelled by the Romans. They survived the Eagle Empire to graft on to the later Norsemen, who had adopted the Fells as their home and indeed gave them their name. That Norse–British splicing could well be the racial bedding of this land, as strong as the slate beneath the turf.

The power of the place though is not yet exhausted, for it was here that Western Europe discovered a laboratory of the mind in nature. The great passion for nature, that enormous change in appreciation and imagination which decided to turn to the once hostile, once barbaric, once despised and merely looted landscape as the place in which we could discover ourselves in the largest and deepest sense, executed much of its early drama here. Daniel Defoe, for instance, on his tour of the British Isles in the eighteenth century, sensed the new mood immediately. It was a perilous place, he reported, dangerous, a wilderness, horrendous; and, he implied, ripe to be tamed. He had written *Robinson Crusoe* in much the same vein: modern enlightened man was to go out to the wilderness in a spirit of conquest but would remain there only because of the power of his curiosity and the new conviction that nature had to be understood, to be treated as an associate – even, as time went on, a wiser, better, superior teacher.

Where Defoe led, the hacks and print-makers, the poets and scientific investigators of the landscape, the roving scholarly clergymen and the nomadic poets followed. The great and initially romantic movement to Naturalism had begun. In this Lakeland landscape was discovered material for speculaton on the origin of the planet – not in theology, but in geology – and

BUTTERMERE AND CRUMMOCK WATER FROM FLEETWITH PIKE

DEERGARTH HOW ISLAND, THIRLMERE

ESKDALE FROM HARD KNOTT

on the sensibility of humankind. Perhaps most influential of all, it was here that Wordsworth preached the healing force of nature and its appropriateness as a source of morality:

> One impulse from a vernal wood
> May teach you more of man,
> Of much evil and of good,
> Than all the sages can.

As the nineteenth century progressed, more and more disciplines and impulses found the Lakes to be an ideal testing ground – literally, indeed, in the case of those who, about a hundred years ago, invented the sport of rock climbing here. Landscape as a subject for painters overtook religion, mythological and historical subjects with astounding swiftness; the country and all things natural became increasingly revered as the main-spring of health, physical, mental, spiritual, even religious.

All these voices are still heard. As you walk across the Fells they filter through your mind, a mind already satiated with the subtlety and the splendours of this lovely and varied place. There is nowhere in my experience like it.

GRAINS GILL, SEATHWAITE

Recently constructed motorways have brought the beauty and the peace of the Lake District within one and a half hour's drive of thousands of Lancastrians and Yorkists and within weekend distance of many more Londoners. Consequently the area has now become one of the most heavily visited mountain playgrounds in Europe. This is creating problems which profoundly affect the wildlife and natural features it embraces. The first and most obvious problem is feet.

The small National Trust property of Tarn Hows, for example, can receive 250 vehicles at a time, bringing so many people to a confined space that there is real danger of their trampling it to destruction. For experiments have shown that if more than about 10,000 people walk over the same piece of turf in a year (and that is less than thirty a day) the surface will break, the soil will be exposed and erosion will follow. As the path becomes loose and muddy, walkers spread further over the terrain, widening the area of erosion. Even where the turf remains intact around the edges its character is altered: very few species tolerate continual trampling, and only plantains and daisies, with their leathery leaves which hug the ground, may survive.

In lowland Britain temporary exclusion of the public results in rapid natural regeneration of the sward, but on the thin, poor, wet soils of the mountains growth is slow. Regeneration may take several years, so firm decisions have to be taken either to close paths or to provide alternative routes.

Millions of visitors also, sadly, bring in their wake a litter problem. Not only does litter disfigure the landscape, it also pollutes and alters it. Plants of the open moor are replaced by nettles and docks and other species that flourish in 'well-fed' soils. This process is aggravated in the absence of toilets, but even where these are provided they only transfer the problem to the lakes: water so enriched increases algal growth which blankets and kills many submerged flowering plants.

Even on remoter crags the weight of numbers is destructive. Sheer cliffs are a challenge to climbers ever keen to seek new routes rather than queue for those already over-subscribed. The climbers inevitably disturb nesting birds such as peregrines and ravens, and if they do not themselves uproot rare alpine plants they may open the way for collectors to reach the previously inaccessible.

These same crags attract scores of geologists, and many of their fine rock exposures are literally taking a hammering as collectors search for fossil starfish and brachiopods.

With pressures on such a scale conservation organizations, many of which have among their objectives education and enjoyment, are faced with a problem. How can they continue to keep their reserves open when the visitors are destroying the very treasures which the reserves were created to protect? Yet how can they put up 'Private – keep out' notices without turning against them the public whose support they need if they are to protect endangered sites? This dilemma must be resolved, but nowhere in Britain is it more pressing than in the Lakes.

HONISTER PASS

THE HIGHLANDS

IAIN CRICHTON SMITH

The Mountain

In summer the deer are questionmarks on the mountains
feeding among the cress.
Their antlers burn in the sunrise.

I have drunk water so sweet
that it was the wine of the wind
brewed in quiet hollows.

We have climbed to where the eagle turns
negligently towards a cloud
with its freight of meat,
and awkward among scree we have slithered
from peak to peak.

I have felt your sweet bones, mountains,
like the bones of a cat,
and sometimes in an autumn evening
the untethered moon drifts.

STOB DEARG FROM THE RIVER COUPALL, STRATHCLYDE

In winter you are white maps,
ice triangles.
The birds and herbs have been squeezed out of
your chained kingdom
where the rivers are quiet
and your skin is an amazing
naturalized ghost.

The green forgets itself.
There is a symmetry
of cruel perfection,
aristocratic, brutal,
an upthrust of eternal
peremptory music.

Startled, we gaze
into the kingdom of the dead,
these peaks of absence
where all has been changed to silence
and the chimes cannot be heard
of these congruent crests.

Argyll

Rowan trees, birches, roses, and calm lochs,
to you Columba came,
imperialist of the spirit, with his books.
This is a rich land, not monkish,
a theatre of the wild.

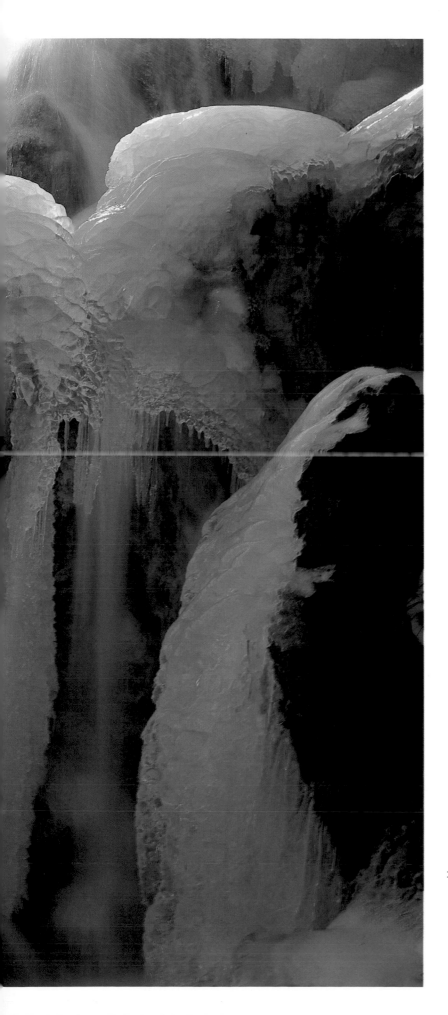

THE RIVER AFFRIC, GLEN AFFRIC, HIGHLAND

LOCHAN AN DAIM, TAYSIDE

LOCHAN NA H-ACHLAISE, RANNOCH MOOR, STRATHCLYDE

STOB NAN CABER, GLEN COE, HIGHLAND

The buzzard rests on the wire, the rabbit
marries the stoat's ring,
and on the hills with their fine scholarly heads
I see my elegant deer.
The wise salmon slides downstream.
The fox burns in the frost.
The trees create a technicolour autumn
in orange and in gold.

Glencoe, you are I think the only weeper
for that winter massacre
assassination on the frozen lochs,
the quick jab of the knife.
But otherwise the rowan berries shine,
an astronomy of wounds,
and waters reflect hills exactly
in their mild immobile glass.
The pheasant like a stained-glass window stalks
proudly among your fields,
illuminated missal, rainbow bird.
And in the Holy Loch the missiles sleep
like rows of organ pipes.

After my bleak island I adore
the largesse of your fruit,
the bramble berries mapping gloveless hands,
the ballet of your birch,
the sea that shines to Islay and Tiree,
to Iona and to Coll.

Such jewellery you have, my calm Argyll,
mild dowager of tales.

You might think, pausing as you climb to look at the peaks all round you, with not another being in sight, that the Highlands remain the last great wilderness in Britain. But it is an illusion, for they are already in the process of being destroyed.

Those native red deer silhouetted majestically against the skyline have spent most of the day in the small remnant of deciduous woodland which follows the course of the burn, browsing on saplings which will never become trees, and condemning the wood to a lingering death.

Now the herd, too large for the land left after afforestation has fenced off the lower ground, is grazing and trampling a steep grass and heather slope, breaking the surface of the sward. In winter, water will penetrate and turn to ice, heaving earth to the surface which will be washed away in the spring rains. Gradually the whole slope will lose its cover, and acres of bare scree will join the others which already scar the landscape. Uncontrolled deer are an ecological disaster.

The solitary silence is shattered by the high whine of a Land Rover following the route of a brash new road which jars the rounded contours and leads to an unmajestic metal mast conveying TV pictures of unspoilt landscapes to isolated crofters. Where one rover leads others follow, illegally on wheels or legally on foot, disturbing the wildlife.

Some summits are too steep for roads but thought fit for skis. On the far side of that mountain to the north a chair-lift is being erected. In winter thousands of Coke-can carriers will line its crest before plunging downwards – too often on snow so thin that the fragile turf is further damaged. In summer more chairpersons are lifted aloft to wander and trample, bringing dangers to rare species once protected by their remoteness.

The dying woodland, eroded slopes, ugly roads, obtrusive masts and litter are obvious to the seeing eye but other, hidden forces which are equally damaging are at work all round.

There are no eagles now riding the wind above the crag which once concealed their eyrie. They have been poisoned by shepherds who wrongly supposed they lifted living lambs when all they took was carrion. Peregrine populations, recovering elsewhere after the ban on organochlorine pesticides as sheep-dips, have not risen here. At night the egg-collectors have used the new road for a quick trip to rob their nest.

There are no living trout in the burn below, for acid rain has been falling, releasing into the water toxic aluminium which attacks the gills of the fish, leaving them to die from lack of oxygen.

The return from the wilderness is now much quicker than it was: spurred on by subsidies from public funds, farmers and foresters are taming the lower slopes, ploughing, reseeding and planting, and thus destroying the moorland.

While you paused the wilderness diminished. If we do not rouse ourselves to combat the dangers, the wildness and the wildlife will disappear as swiftly as those deer which have now slipped silently over the brow.

LOCH LURGAINN AND STAC POLLAIDH, HIGHLAND

ORKNEY

GEORGE MACKAY BROWN

It is best perhaps to come to the islands in midsummer; then the late-setting sun dips under the north-west horizon only briefly, to rise a few hours later in the north-east. The sun-glow never leaves the north.

In that glimmering enchanted twilight the farms lie sleeping in valleys and along the sea shore. The fields with their increasing burden of ripeness, and the animals, lie with the blessing of dew on them. The tilth lands and pasture seem timeless, as if they were from everlasting to everlasting. The quiet skies, waters, hills, have the quality of ancient heraldry.

It is a people contented and at peace. You can tell that from the slow unhurried lilt of the country speech.

It was not always that way.

Many small wars, raids and plunderings and stormings, went to create that peace.

Summertime Orkney is not the whole truth. Come in midwinter, and taste another kind of magic – the dark storms that fling spindrift higher than the crags and lace with stinging salt the links. The great tempest of January 1952 blew henhouses out to sea, cockerels raging aloft. The long winter darkness has a different heraldry: stars, the changing orb of the moon, occasionally (between gales) the beautiful dance of the aurora borealis in the north.

BAY OF HOUTON, MAINLAND, ORKNEY

CRAIG GATE FROM RACK WICK, HOY

Edwin Muir, himself the son of an Orkney farmer, but long a stranger to the islands, rediscovered them in his Scottish journey in the mid-1930s. Orkney seemed to him then the most prosperous and contented community in a Scotland racked by economic and industrial stagnation. Childhood memories had provided him with the symbol of Eden that he uses with such luminous power in his verse.

Nothing much has changed in the fifty years since *Scottish Journey*. But it is impossible to appreciate the Orkney of today without the dimension of history. We are the mingled weave that many hands have worked on.

The feet of many strangers have visited the islands in the course of six thousand years or so, and have stayed, compelled by a magic that is still operant. (Orkney has two opposed effects on strangers; either it attracts them strongly, or else they take one appalled look and turn away.)

What human foot first touched a shore here, after the slow retreat of the ice, no one can now say. In the island of Papay has been recently unearthed the oldest dwelling-house in Europe. It is strange to think of those remote ancestors drinking the same wind, measuring with eye and oar the same tides as ourselves. What their thoughts and speech were, no one will ever know. The harshness of their circumstance meant that they probably did not live long; a man was old when he was in his thirties. They were delicate and marked for an early death. But what amazing courage, to set out from the north coast or the west coast of Scotland, to the islands that lay further north still, dark and glimmering on the water like sleeping whales. For their boats were as light and delicate as themselves, and the sleeve of sea they had to cross was the Pentland Firth, one of the world's wildest sea-passages. Not only themselves had to embark, but the livestock on which they depended had to be laid, bound and bolt-eyed, in the ships. So they stepped ashore, on Hoy or on Ronaldsay; and the skippers eyed with dismay the weave of heather and fern everywhere. But the poet of the tribe put beauty of harp and voice on the new place, a beseechment or a coercion. Within that poem of increase we still perhaps live, though the words of the chant are lost.

SEAWEED, WAULKMILL BAY, MAINLAND

The poem of greeting and welcome first, then the settlement, the clearing of land for the plough (if those early ones had knowledge of agriculture at all), the probing of the sea for fish, the building of a larger house for the chief than for the others (stone it had to be, for the place had few trees). Nor did they neglect to build a chamber of death for those who died that first winter: the very old and the very young, and the girl who, racked with seasickness on the terrible crossing, never got her strength back.

'Brief, brutish, and nasty' perhaps: but through the wretched weave runs the red thread of courage.

The poet sang silver elegies at the end of that first winter.

The whole story of the islands is a repetition, with variations, of that first coming.

Those discoverers were not suffered to dwell unmolested in their valley, or on the margin of their bay, where the soil was sweetened with blown shell-sand. The same urge that had driven them to break the horizon northwards brought sequent tribes, possibly of the same basic stock as themselves – then the shore stones were splashed with blood, the caves echoed with rage and defiance.

Invasion, uprooting again and again and again: until at last a skilled ruthless people established themselves; and probably their old chief was in his forties (so much higher the cornstalk grew). And at his long table the harvested corn, changed to bread and ale, was broken in peace. *They* would not easily be chased from their acres. But what is a hundred years, or even three centuries, in the eye of time? Other stronger north-farers took over the fields and the fishing boats, the stones of the township too were reddened. A new chamber of death was opened, with reverence, to receive the wounds and the stillness.

And another poet harped and cried over the conquered glebe.

These are but conjectures, pictures of the past in a twentieth-century imagination.

There came to Orkney a people who had curiosity about the movement of sun and stars and planets, to whom the winter night-skies were a perpetual wonderment. At Brodgar, between the two lochs, they sought to capture the subtle movements of the stars in a stone web. The stones of divination are still there, in a wide circle, a few of them broken down and eroded by centuries of lightning, storms, rain. The stones at Brodgar may have been fertility symbols, to ensure ripeness of corn and of animals. They might – so daring and ingenious those people – have symbolized a first groping towards the mysteries of time and eternity; for a circle has no beginning and no end.

Near the two stone henges of Stenness and Brodgar lies the most magnificent stone-built burial chamber of all: Maeshowe. It was as if all the little honeycombs of death built by the earlier tribes had in Maeshowe their majestic consummation. Death, the end of all things living? The poet-architects of Maeshowe had so arranged their chamber that the midwinter sun, as it sets over the Coolag hill of Hoy, sends a fleeting beam through the long corridor and makes a splash of gold on the opposite wall. It is seen, that marvellous symbol, only on the few afternoons clustered about the dark solstice.

There came a people, possibly early Celts, and took possession of the islands; they built primitive stone keeps, or castles, along the shores and beside the lochs. Those brochs were marvellous edifices against the weaponry of the time. They were not built for fun; the sea-borne tribes were still moving west and north, seeking, through violence, the cornstalk and the fish that were (on the long table) symbols of peace at last. But now the Orkneymen knew how to defend themselves. The whole township, in times of trouble, was closed inside the impregnable broch, each with its animals and children. They endured, between the fire and the well of sweet water, until the besiegers got disheartened and sailed away, a few with bruises and burn marks on them, and the mocking satire of the Aikerness poet echoing still in their ears.

The old chief – who might now, near death, be in his early fifties (higher still grew the cornstalk), herded the people out to their unconquered fields and shores.

HOY FROM MAINLAND

PEAT HEATH, QUEEFIGLAMO

The Picts came, and left a few enigmatic stone carvings, and ploughed out more bog and heather . . .

Now the Orkneymen expected invasion to come always from Scotland or the Hebrides; only from those airts the perennial danger.

The Norsemen broke into Orkney from the east – first as pirates and raiders, but at last as settlers, for they could see well enough how the land had been tamed and made fertile by the plough and the ox, the sun and the rain and the seed.

They were so contemptuous of the settled Picts that they did not even bother to mention them in *The Orkneyinga Saga,* that marvellous record of the history of Orkney over three centuries. In no time these blond warriors in their beautiful dragon-headed ships possessed the islands utterly. A line of magnificent Viking earls ruled Orkney and Shetland. There was Earl Sigurd, who led his Orkneymen to the Battle of Clontarf in Ireland, in 1014, under the death-bringing, victory-bringing raven banner woven by his mother; Earl Thorfinn the Mighty – Macbeth's kinsman – who ruled nine earldoms in Scotland and was more powerful than the King of Scotland himself; the two joint earls, Hakon and Magnus, whose intersecting graphs came together and were sealed in blood in the island of Egilsay, and who fared forth again, Hakon to a peaceful and plenteous rule over a contented folk, and the soul of the martyred St Magnus 'to the fair pastures of heaven' (the great cathedral of St Magnus still stands, where many miracles of healing took place); the most attractive character in the Saga, Earl Rognvald – chevalier, poet, pilgrim to Jerusalem, 'master of nine crafts', whose golden days were ended by violence at a farm in Caithness; and the lesser earls, with whom the story peters out.

A brave tapestry they wove, the Norse Orkneymen.

Then came the Scots as rulers, administrators, taxmen; and it was 'the end of an old song'. The nine earldoms shrank to an unimportant group of Scottish islands, fair game for the plucking.

So Orkney entered a dark age lasting many centuries, with only a gleam here and there.

RING OF BRODGAR, MAINLAND

Our near ancestors endured a long age of oppression and misrule. The dark stubborn earth they worked was grained into them – sea salt was in their veins. They endured, and now their great-grandchildren move and work in quieter times and reap a moderate prosperity (it is no unusual thing for Orkney men and women to live into their eighties and nineties: so much time the tall oats and barley yielded them).

The medieval village of Kirkwall grew beside St Magnus Cathedral. Today it is the capital city – the prosperous mercantile and administrative heart of Orkney. The only other town, Stromness, is wedded to the sea. Adventurers and skippers move through its briefer history, all salt yarns and gulls and tar.

There are a handful of villages in this island and that, with shop and kirk and pub.

But still the real Orkney is to be found in the farm-steadings and houses 'sunk deep in time', with the heraldries of corn and beast, and the Atlantic fish . . . All around, the brown and green hills rise and fall like waves.

How much longer?

No community stands still. Today is a kind of small golden age for Orkney, without heroes or saints (who tend to show themselves only in times of peril and distress).

Oil has been found in the North Sea off Orkney; but the terminal and tanks and ships are confined to one island in Scapa Flow: Flotta.

It is known for a certainty that the soil of Orkney is moderately rich with uranium ore. The Orcadians – people slow to enthusiasm or indignation – closed ranks a few years ago when there was a move to make probes under their acres.

Earth-gold, sea-silver: these have been the signs on our heraldic shield, for many centuries now.

The islands have never been slow to welcome new things – field enclosures, machines, piped water, electricity – once they have convinced themselves that the innovations will lighten their yoke.

But from this element that has been waiting under their furrows from the

LOCH OF STENNESS, MAINLAND

beginning, they turn away, they have nothing to say about it, they feel it to be more alien and dangerous than the first bronze axe laid on the stones of Skarabrae. Concerning uranium, the poets and artists are silent, or they put a warning finger to their lips. (How could there ever be an ode to uranium?)

But nowadays the voice of art is drained of its ancient power, as we leave the age of the word and are gathered – whether we like it or not – into a bleak grey time when 'the number' will compel our goings and comings, and the good heraldry over our doors is a blank.

There was a time when fluctuations in the population of plants and animals on our shores and in the seas around us were controlled by storms and tides, exceptional frosts or prolonged droughts, and our modest harvesting of fish, fowl or laver-bread had only local, short-term effects. But all that changed with the growth of the oil industry. The transport of millions of tons of a poisonous and buoyant liquid in vulnerable vessels of ever increasing size across oceans and through congested coastal waters to terminals in enclosed harbours, has produced a threat to the wildlife of the four-fifths of our globe which are seas and oceans and all the coasts which border them.

This threat is intensified when the origin of the oil is the sea-bed itself and the wells and terminals are closely congregated, as around the northern isles of Orkney and Shetland. The threat became a reality at Christmas 1978 when fuel oil spilt from the *Esso Bernicia* in Sullom Voe, Shetland, killing at least a dozen otters and injuring many more, and oiling thousands of sea birds, especially awks such as guillemots and razorbills, the majority condemned to a lingering death.

Oil damages the plumage of sea birds, allowing water to penetrate the air spaces between the feathers and skin so that they lose buoyancy and sink. Even if they do not drown, the removal of an insulating layer of air causes such a rapid loss of heat that they soon exhaust their body reserves. With their natural food also polluted they die of starvation, a death accelerated by the toxic effects of ingested oil which damages their liver and kidneys as they try to clean their feathers by preening. The most sophisticated bird rescue centres can do little to clean and rehabilitate badly oiled birds in large numbers, and the only humane act is to destroy them.

Many techniques have been tried to limit damage by oil pollution. Some physical methods in the open sea or on sandy beaches are effective but the chemicals used, especially in confined spaces, have often caused more harm than the oil itself. Coasts such as rocky shores and saltmarshes are almost impossible to clean up: the effect of an oil spill may last for decades.

The best solution to oil pollution is prevention. An obvious and necessary move is the installation of sophisticated navigational aids and electronic devices in tankers to reduce the chance of accidents. Recent figures show however that the largest part of pollution by tankers does not arise from collisions but from the way they are operated – for example, the washing out of tanks at sea. With satellite surveillance of the world it should surely soon be possible for unlawful pollution by tankers to be recorded and reported so that the guilty can be punished by an international court. Clean seas are vital to the future of marine wildlife, and only determined action on an international scale can prevent further destruction of their living resources.

THE OLD MAN OF HOY

Acknowledgments

The authors would like to thank the following for
their valuable assistance in making this book possible:

Anaheim City School District, Deputy Superintendent
William A. Thompson, Coordinator of Special Education,
Ann Beavers and the Special Education staff for their
support and concern for children with special needs;

Debora Skarshaug Crowley, OTR/L; Mary Jane
Zehnpfennig, MA, OTR; Babetta Velategui, MOT, OTR;
and Carol Hamilton, MA, OTR for their critical input
and encouragement;

Stephen Leinau and Sensory Integration International
for their recognition of the value of our work to the larger
professional community in publishing this manual;

Irene Bagge and The Stairwell Group for their indis-
pensable guidance throughout the production process.

Contents

Sensory and Motor Components

Trouble Shooting

Ball and Balloon Games

Bean Bag Games

Games With Easily Made Equipment

Games Without Equipment

Jump Rope Games

Tool Activities

Appendix

Bibliography

Dedicated to A. Jean Ayres, PhD, OTR, FAOTA

Preface

Occupational therapists, teachers, and parents are constantly searching for resources to help children who experience difficulties in the classroom. The authors of this book are occupational therapists with experience in education and knowledge of the neurological principles underlying the development of sensory processing and motor performance as they relate to learning and behavior. They have written this fully illustrated manual, purposely avoiding medical terminology, to assist those who are working with children in special education.

Problems in the development of attention, direction-following, creative imagination, eye-hand coordination, self-esteem, and social appropriateness are often observed in a child with special needs and can sometimes be related to faulty perception of sensory information. When faced with developmental delays, sensory processing problems, or poor motor coordination, therapists and teachers need to identify the "just right" activity — the ones that *really* work — to meet the varied needs of these children.

The activities selected have been tried and proven successful in a variety of situations ranging from regular education classrooms to those which serve the multiple handicapped. The suggested activities are easy to implement, require a minimal amount of equipment, and will create fun and memorable childhood experiences.

This book provides teachers with a framework from which to observe, modify, and implement motor-related activities in the classroom. It is to be used by occupational therapists as a springboard for the many classroom activity analyses that they can so uniquely provide. It was created with great care for this purpose.

Sensory and Motor Components Related to Learning and Behavior

The basic sensory and motor components which influence learning and behavior are defined and described in this section. These components, in alphabetical order, are:

- Auditory Processing
- Body Awareness
- Coordinating Body Sides
- Fine Motor Control
- Motor Planning
- Ocular Control
- Perception of Movement
- Perception of Touch
- Visual-Spatial Perception

Through an understanding of the significance of these sensory and motor components a teacher will be better able to recognize factors which may be promoting success or causing failure in the classroom.

Auditory Processing

Auditory processing is the perception of and ability to understand what is heard in the environment. This involves more than the sense of hearing. Understanding auditory information requires processes such as the ability to discriminate between sounds, to associate and decode sounds, and to remember what is heard.

Auditory processing plays an important role in a child's classroom performance. A child that experiences difficulty processing what is heard may at times appear confused or inattentive. He may haphazardly rush into a task and may take a long time to respond to directions and complete tasks. He may not be able to sufficiently block out competing background noise. Remembering and sequencing multiple step directions may require added concentration and effort. Good auditory processing is an important foundation for development of language.

Processing auditory information is believed to begin before birth and to continue throughout life. Long before a child can attach meaning to the spoken word or talk, auditory processing has begun. A young infant will give a response to a sudden loud noise or to his mother's voice, although he can only interpret these sounds as threatening or pleasurable. As the child matures, he interprets a variety of sounds and words and learns to respond appropriately. His response becomes more selective and he learns to block out irrelevant sounds around him. The twelve-month-old child understands much of what is said and heard. Songs, rhymes, storytelling, and listening and response games stimulate auditory processing and language comprehension in normal development.

Body Awareness

Awareness of one's body comes from sensations from muscles and joints. Receptors located in the muscles and joints tell the brain when and how the muscles are contracting or stretching and when and how the joints are bending, extending, or being pulled and compressed. This information enablaes the brain to know where each part of the body is and how it is moving through space without looking.

The muscles, joints, and brain provide each other with vital sensory information to make spatial and temporal adjustments possible in movement. Integration of this information enables the child to execute gross and fine motor activities that require subtle variations in posture, strength, force, and dexterity. A child with poor awareness of body parts tends to rely on visual information and may not be able to move properly if he cannot see where his arms and legs are. Without this visual information, he may fall out of his seat. He may have a vague awareness of his position in space and have a difficult time getting dressed or into and out of a car.

A child with poor body awareness may have difficulty knowing where his body is in relation to objects. He frequently breaks toys because he does not know how much pressure he is exerting when putting things together or pulling things apart. He may have poor fine motor control because he cannot accurately feel where or how his arm, forearm, hand, or fingers are moving and does not have precise information about the tool in his hand. He typically presses too hard or too softly with a pencil. A child with a problem in this area may appear sloppy, clumsy, or have disorganized personal belongings.

Information regarding body awareness is provided to the brain when muscles and joints are working against gravity or resistance. This occurs normally in development when a child crawls, climbs, lifts, and carries heavy objects or pushes and pulls objects such as push toys and wagons with resistance.

4

Coordinating Body Sides

The ability to coordinate the right and left sides of the body and to cross the midline of the body is an indication that both sides of the brain are working well together and sharing information efficiently. Coordination of the two body sides is an important foundation for the development of many gross and fine motor skills. It is essential to the development of cerebral specialization for skilled use of a dominant hand.

A child with poor coordination of the two body sides may adjust his body to avoid crossing the midline. He may not be able to coordinate one hand to move while the other hand is acting as an assist to stabilize the project. He may switch hands during a fine motor task because he is experiencing frustration with skillfully using his hands together.

Good coordination of the two body sides is an important foundation for writing with pencils and cutting with scissors. The ability to coordinate the two body sides is first observed when a baby transfers objects from one hand to another, bangs two blocks together or imitates pat-a-cake. Children learn to coordinate their body sides when they manipulate toys such as pop beads and leggos, and when they skip, gallop, play rhythm games, jump rope, or ride a bike.

Fine Motor Control

Fine motor control is the ability to precisely utilize one's hands and fingers in a skilled activity. Good fine motor skill stems from solid sensory and motor foundations. For good fine motor control, it is important to have muscle and joint stability, especially in the neck, trunk, and upper extremities. One's eye muscles must work in a coordinated manner to quickly localize and track objects in the environment and smoothly guide the hand. Subconscious awareness of where and how hands and fingers are moving in space, accurate tactile discrimination and hand strength aid in the control of objects of various sizes, weights, shapes, and textures. The ability to accurately judge the visual spatial relationship of objects is essential for the precision required in fine motor control. The ability to motor plan, that is organize and carry out a sequence of unfamiliar motor tasks, is involved in many fine motor activities. Coordination of the two sides of the body is essential to fine motor coordination and the development of hand dominance.

Hand use developmentally precedes tool use. Through a progression of hand movements the child gradually acquires the precision needed for fine motor skill with tools. The following is a brief overview of the significance and development of hand control.

GROSS GRASP

The progression of early grasp patterns begins with the use of the whole hand from a raking approach to a palmar grasp which uses the fingers to press the object against the palm. The thumb then becomes incorporated into the grasp pattern.

The whole hand is used to "hang on" to the object without isolating the use of various fingers. Strength of grasp becomes a critical factor as the infant becomes mobile. A secure grasp is part of the foundation for pulling up to the standing position. It enables the child to secure objects for climbing, pushing, and pulling. Grasp is challenged when a child hangs on to ropes when swinging, hangs from monkey bars or plays *Tug of War*.

GROSS RELEASE

Developmentally, the ability to grasp and hold an object is followed by a gross release. Initially, release is crude and somewhat random. Refining the ability to release enables the child to have greater control over objects. A child practices and refines his ability to release through play as he grasps and lets go of toys. Opportunities in play to stack blocks, put things in containers, and to toss bean bags or balls help refine these skills.

FINE GRASP

Fine grasp is characterized by the ability to control each finger independently and in relation to the thumb. This is evident as the child learns to point his index finger, pokes at objects, and picks up small objects. The child then incorporates the middle finger into his pinch pattern, which provides him with a more secure fine grasp pattern. Skill and dexterity in using fine grasp is challenged as the child finger feeds and plays with pegs, beads, and crayons. Pre-writing skills emerge.

TIMED GRASP AND RELEASE

Once a child has practiced grasp and release in a random fashion, an element of timing emerges. Timing refers to choosing an appointed or fixed moment for something to happen, begin or end. Timing a motor response is a critical component of hand dexterity. Timing is developed in a gross motor sense when a child motor plans the actions of his whole body. In fine motor activities, timing for fine motor precision is practiced when a child uses eating utensils, throws and catches bean bags and balls, and begins to use a variety of tools.

HAND DOMINANCE

Many children who have fine motor problems may not have established hand dominance. Genetics, sensory processing and overall motor coordination can affect the development of hand dominance.

Genetically a child is thought to be predisposed to developing a preference for one hand over the other for fine motor precision. Inefficient central nervous system processing can interfere with the genetic urge to use a dominant hand. It has been hypothesized (Ayres, DiQuerios) that when a brain is struggling with the interpretation of sensory information, this takes precedence over higher level brain functions such as the development of hand dominance for skilled fine motor control.

Overall motor coordination is an important foundation for the development of hand dominance. Hand dominance can be thought of as an end product of earlier developmental steps. The development of good coordination between the two body sides and the ability to plan, time, and sequence an activity gives a child confidence to rely on one hand more dominantly for tasks requiring precision. A child who has the opportunity to develop solid sensory and motor foundations may automatically establish hand dominance.

TOOL CONTROL

Before a child can use tools in a coordinated manner, he must have basic control over his hands. The development of a gross grasp is important to overall strength and stability when holding the tool. Fine grasp is necessary to allow each finger and the thumb to accommodate to a wide variety of tools. The overall ability to coordinate the body sides is essential to provide stability with one hand while the other hand is engaged in a task requiring precision in movement. Timing of grasp and release and motor planning ability are important to execute quick yet accurate control over tools.

9

Motor Planning

Motor planning is the ability of the brain to conceive of, organize and carry out a sequence of unfamiliar actions. Motor planning is the first step in learning new skills. Good motor planning ability requires accurate information from all sensory systems of the body.

Sensations from the eyes, ears, skin, muscle and joints and from the vestibular system provide the brain with basic and essential information. This information is important in order to be able to organize sensory impulses to plan, organize, time, and sequence an unfamiliar task. If a basic sensory component is contributing faulty or slow information, motor planning ability could be seriously compromised.

A child with poor motor planning may seem clumsy, accident prone, and messy. He may experience a prolonged period of struggle in attempting to master a new skill and, therefore, establish routines for himself to eliminate the need for unfamiliar movement. A bright child may be able to compensate for his lack of accurate sensory information by figuring out the demands of a task cognitively but may expend undue mental energy in doing so. A child of average intelligence may spend his time minding another child's business, and may be verbally manipulative in order to avoid having to perform motorically. This child may imitate the actions of another child rather than try to initiate the activity himself. Another child may even experience difficulty imitating the actions of others and find it difficult to follow a teacher's visual instructions.

Motor planning abilities are challenged in the classroom each time a child is presented with a variation of a familiar motor task or with a new assignment. When learning to write or cut with scissors, a child synthesizes a variety of sensory information to plan and sequence each stroke or cut in order to successfully complete the task. A child with a motor planning problem may have significant difficulty finishing his work on time as he does not have an idea of how to start or a strategy for finishing the task. Another child may rush through the task without being able to recognize the parts or steps of the task as they relate to the end product. This child typically turns in messy, haphazard work.

Developmentally, a child learns to motor plan as he is exposed to variations of familiar activities. Through play, a child explores the use of many objects and develops creative ideas for a variety of actions. Motor planning is developed when a child experiments with how parts relate to a whole in such toys as puzzles and simple take-apart toys or models. A child learns to imitate when he plays pat-a-cake, peek-a-boo and later games such as *Simon-Says*, *Mother-May-I*, and *Follow the Leader*. Motor planning is further developed when a child is asked to sequence several motor actions in a new skill or several directions in an unfamiliar task.

Ocular Control

Ocular control is the smooth and coordinated movements of the eyes to attend to and follow objects and people in the environment. Controlled eye movements are needed for finding and tracking a moving object, scanning the environment, sustaining eye contact on a fixed object or person, quickly shifting focus from one thing to another and for eye-hand coordination.

A child with poor ocular control may have difficulty controlling his eyes to follow a moving object. Eye contact while speaking to another person or fixating the eyes on a task may be momentary, making it hard for the child to look at something long enough to process its meaning. The child may not be able to copy assignments from the blackboard to the paper in a reasonable amount of time. He may be unable to coordinate smooth eye movements to read across a line. He may have trouble using his eyes to guide his hands for writing and using tools. The child may try to work with his eyes very close to his paper in an effort to gain better ocular control. This child may also have problems with depth perception if his eyes are not working well symmetrically.

Children refine ocular control developmentally as they are involved in movement activities such as rolling, crawling, and walking in an effort to reach people and objects. Ocular control is challenged in play when children toss and catch balls and bean bags, manipulate toys or use tools.

Perception of Movement

Perception of movement refers to the processing of vestibular information in the brain. The receptors in the inner ear perceive information about the force of gravity and movement. By sending messages to higher centers in the brain, the vestibular system aids in maintaining joint stability, posture, balance, motor control, spatial awareness, and a stable visual field. In addition, the vestibular system sends information to a part of the brain that regulates attention. Therefore, movement can be used to facilitate attention or to provide a calming effect.

Some children may not process enough information about gravity and movement while others "over" process the incoming sensory information. The child who is not processing enough movement information may have trouble stabilizing and coordinating neck and eye musculature in order to copy letters, draw, or follow a line in reading. He may not be able to maintain his posture subconsciously and needs to concentrate on sitting in his chair. He leans heavily on his desk when he is trying to listen to the teacher. When standing in line he looks for someone or something to lean on. He may lose his balance easily or appear to move excessively, using momentum to compensate for poor equilibrium responses.

The child who perceives too much movement information may be overly frightened by movement. He may not be able to keep up with his peers on the playground and has difficulty mastering environmental obstacles such as stairs or uneven terrain. He may become fearful, stubborn or so overly stimulated by movement that he becomes a behavior problem.

Many activities provide opportunities for processing movement information in the brain. Some examples are rolling, running, hopping, skipping, and jumping. Playground equipment such as swings, slides, merry-go-rounds and teeter-totters are good sources of movement experiences. When a teacher observes that a child is having problems with posture, balance or tolerating movement, providing these opportunities may be helpful. If a child appears to fear to seek an excess of movement and this behavior is interfering with independent functioning in the classroom, an occupational therapist should be contacted.

Perception of Touch

Tactile perception pertains to the sense of touch on the skin. The tactile system is a two-fold system involving the interpretation of protective and discriminative information. The protective tactile system is responsible for the body, automatically withdrawing or defending itself from touch that is interpreted as harmful. The discriminative touch system provides the brain with the precise information regarding size, shape, and texture of objects in the environment. The integrity of both tactile systems is essential for tool use and for many aspects of social and emotional development.

A child with a problem related to a disordered tactile system may be hypersensitive or hyposensitive to touch or have poor tactile discrimination. The hypersensitive child may appear aggressive in his interaction with others. He may avoid art projects or outdoor play in the grass, dirt or sand because of his tactile discomfort. His need to protect himself from inadvertent tactile input may result in poor attentional skills. The hyposensitive child may be unaware of being touched and not react normally to painful experiences such as cuts and bruises. The child with poor tactile discrimination may have difficulty manipulating tools and toys.

Activities providing a variety of tactile input include art projects, cooking with different ingredients, going barefoot in the gass, sand or dirt, and games involving different textures and materials. Tactile activities should never be forcefully imposed upon a child who avoids or complains about tactile stimuli. If the teacher suspects that a tactile problem is interfering with tool use, peer relationships or independent functioning in the classroom, and attempts to involve the child in a variety of tactile activities fail, then an occupational therapist should be consulted.

Visual-Spatial Perception

Visual-spatial perception is how a person perceives the relationship of external space to his body as well as how he perceives objects in space relative to other objects. The importance of eyesight in classroom performance is obvious but sight alone is not enough. Vision needs to be combined with an interpretation of the physical environment to gain meaning from what we see.

Visual-spatial perception provides us with information about our environment. The way a child perceives space and his orientation within that space can affect his gross motor skills and classroom performance. Without adequate visual-spatial perception, a child may bump into things and may have difficulty getting from one place to another without getting lost. During team sports he may run toward the wrong goal. Judgment of distance and height may be inadequate. Executing stairs and curbs, pouring from containers, and shooting at targets may be difficult. The formation of letters may be laborious if a child is not able to identify visual and spatial similarities and differences. A child with a problem in this area may not know where to start writing on the paper. His letters may vary in size, spacing, and alignment. Letter and number recognition may be poor and reversal of letters can be a common problem. Copying words from the blackboard onto paper may be difficult. He may have difficulty staying within his personal boundaries and his school supplies and personal belongings may be scattered and disorganized.

Locomotion provides the child with experience to learn about the relationship between himself and the physical environment. As the child explores the space around him, his sense of movement, body awareness, and visual input come together to form an internal map of the relationship between himself, objects, and space. Initially, visual-spatial perception develops as the child moves over, under, through, and around objects in the course of his play. As these experiences are organized in the brain, perceptual areas such as form constancy, position of objects in space, figure-ground, and depth perception begin to emerge. The ability to place cognitive labels on space such as right, left, above, and below requires that these perceptual foundations be well established physically.

Trouble Shooting

Overcoming Sensory-Motor Obstacles
in the Classroom

Children come to school with a wide variety of strengths and limitations. When an assignment is presented to a class of children, there will be many different approaches used in attempting to complete the task. Some children will begin and complete a task with ease. Some children have difficulty staying in their seats or knowing where to begin the task. Other children readily begin an assignment, struggle through the task and never seem to finish. It is the responsibility of the teacher and school district staff to modify activities so that each child experiences success in beginning and completing tasks appropriate for his potential with the least amount of frustration and stress.

Modifying an activity is not an easy task. There are many factors related to successful performance. The accurate perception of movement, touch, body awareness, auditory and visual information, the coordination of eye movements, the coordination of the two body sides, and the execution of a motor plan influence one's ability to perform skillfully without undue effort. The amount of structure provided in the implementation of an activity can influence the productivity of a class. Peer interaction and sportsmanship are additional factors contributing to the success of many activities in the classroom.

Classroom activities can be modified in a number of ways to correspond to a child's sensory and motor needs. The purpose of this chapter is to stimulate a teacher's interest and ability to modify activites. The following pages provide strategies for modifying activities. There are no hard and fast solutions, but have you tried . . . ? (see next page)

Strategies for Modifying Activities

When a child is having difficulty with an activity have you tried . . .

- Weighing the value of that activity? Is it something that the child really needs to master or can he get through school years without this skill?

- Practicing activities with similar demands using other media? Try practicing direction following, listening, independent planning, sequencing, task persistence, and task completion through art projects, music games and motor activities.

- Following developmental progressions? Consult your favorite developmental schedule or evaluation tool to get ideas for adjusting the level of skill expected.

- Progressing from repetition to trial and error problem-solving to abstract problem-solving? Sometimes children need more time for repetition and experimentation.

- Assigning a task that can be completed in a short period of time? Emphasize the completion of a task. Some children have difficulty independently organizing and initiating the parts of the whole task. Try to break the task into parts and document success in completing each part. It is more satisfying to complete several small tasks than to continuously struggle and never quite complete one long task. Some children need to see instant results. Adjust the task so that the child can finish the task in a set amount of time. This will develop a sense of accomplishment and confidence in completing tasks.

- Identifying the importance of the end product to the child? Sometimes the process in completing a task is more important to the child than the end product. Sometimes the end product is very important to the child. Satisfaction builds motivation and persistence.

- Protecting self esteem while gaining the child's attention? Provide a silent way of signaling a child who is inattentive. Try a gentle tap on the shoulder or a cue card placed on the child's desk.

- Providing consistent positive and negative consequences to motivate students?

- Presenting instructions both visually and auditorily?

- Analyzing desk and chair size? Feet should rest comfortably on the floor. Knees should not touch the desk. The eyes should be an elbow length above the desk. To check desk size, have the child place his elbow on the desk and rest his chin on his fist.

- Adding or subtracting sensory information? When analyzing a task, check the environment for auditory, visual, and tactile distractions. Consider classroom arrangement and seating.

The following pages provide examples of ways to add or subtract sensory information.

Beginning And Completing Tasks

Problems In This Area Could Be Related To:

Have you tried • • •

AUDITORY PROCESSING

Difficulty understanding and interpreting the spoken word can interfere with a child's ability to begin and complete a task.

- Giving one direction at a time? Sometimes, if a child is given a three-part command, he will act on only the last direction.

- Using short, simple, one-concept phrases to give directions? Do not elaborate. Repeat verbal directions slowly, firmly, clearly.

- Waiting? Wait a little longer than you think is necessary to give the child time to analyze the command and put it into action.

- Giving a visual demonstration or physical assistance?

- Reducing auditory distractions? Be aware of papers shuffling, pencils dropping, etc. Provide ear mufflers.

- Scheduling classroom activities with high auditory processing demands at a time when auditory competition outside is at a minimum?

- Practicing verbal direction-following in gross motor games? Progress from one- to four-step sequences.

- Insisting that a child does not move until you have finished the direction? Have the child repeat the direction in the proper sequence.

MOTOR PLANNING

The ability to plan, organize and sequence strategics is essential to beginning and completing tasks.

- Helping the child identify steps needed to begin and accomplish the task? Have the student repeat directions and, if possible, write down the steps.

- Giving a short assignment so that a child can feel instant success in completing a task? Document the length of time a child can focus on one task and structure the assignment so that it can be completed in that length of time. Try a sand timer to pace work.

- A system for checking off steps as they are accomplished?

- Giving one direction at a time? After one action is successfully completed, add another direction.

- Helping the child physically move through the action?

- Minimizing visual distractions? Check for clutter in classroom environment. Provide a study carrel.

- Art projects that require assemblying parts to create an object? This challenges the student's ability to develop strategies for organizing parts as they relate to the whole.

- Playing *Simon Says* and games that require imitation to see if the student is able to process directions and copy?

Problems In This Area Could Be Related To:

Have you tried • • •

OCULAR CONTROL

Weak eye muscles can make eyes tire easily when they are required to repeatedly shift focus from the blackboard to the desk.

- Writing small amounts on blackboard at a time?

- Alternating blackboard activities with less visually demanding tasks?

- Scheduling a few moments to close and relax eyes between tasks?

- Eye tracking activities such as suspended ball, balloon, and bean bag games? These games challenge the alternating focus from near to far. Try to have the target approximately the same distance as a blackboard is to a seat.

- Wheelbarrow walking and rolling games? These activities help strengthen eye, head, and neck stability important for a stable visual field.

- Checking for dull or flickering lights?

- Eliminating art objects that dangle from the ceiling? Movement can be distracting and can interfere with the processing of visual information.

VISUAL — SPATIAL PERCEPTION

Unidentified acuity problems as well as difficulty transferring visual-spatial information across two visual planes can make copying from the blackboard difficult.

- Checking with parents and school nurse to see if there is an acuity problem?

- A clean blackboard? Yellow chalk is thought to have the best visibility.

- An easel with large white paper and a thick black magic marker?

- An overhead projector so that you can visually isolate different words or sentences?

- Copying from one paper to another— in the same plane?

- Providing the child with a ditto outline of material to be covered on a blackboard? Until a child is independent in copying, try having portions of blackboard material already on his paper.

- Reducing the amount of copying expected? The time it takes for some children to copy compromises the time that a child could spend thinking and responding. Provide photocopies of material which would otherwise have to be copied.

- Teaching strategies for remembering whole words, phrases or sentences at one glance? Sometimes copying is done in a tedious letter by letter manner.

Problems In This Area Could Be Related To:

Have you tried • • •

COORDINATING BODY SIDES

Cutting with scissors requires one hand to guide while the other hand cuts. Both hands must work well together.

- Providing opportunities for the right and left arms and hands to work together? Try clapping and lummi stick games.

- Providing opportunity for hands and fingers to practice working together? Try leggo, pop bead, tinker toy, bead stringing, sewing, and woodworking projects.

- Paper folding and paper tearing as part of art projects?

- Mixing bowl activities so that one hand stabilizes the bowl and the other hand mixes? Try sand and water or food mixes. For tool variation, try a spoon, whip, egg beater, fork.

FINE MOTOR CONTROL

A tool is only as accurate as the hands and fingers that control it.

- Hand grasp strengthening activities? For example, holding on to the ropes of swings, playing tug-of-war, using a hole punch, spraying with trigger-type spray bottles can help strengthen grasp.

- Providing opportunities for practicing timed grasp and release with tools other than scissors? Try using tweezers or tongs to sort cotton balls, blocks, play dough balls, lentils, etc.

- Cutting without a demand for precision? Try cutting pieces of straws, grass, strips of paper, rolls of play dough.

- Consulting a resource for appropriate developmental expectations? Developmentally, children are not ready for scissors until approximately five years of age.

Problems In This Area Could Be Related To:

Have you tried • • •

BODY AWARENESS

Some children with poor awareness of where, how, and with what force their body parts are moving may inadvertently run into their peers or play too roughly.

- Markers at the door? Space markers can be made by placing sticker dots or masking tape lines for each child to stand on while waiting.

- Having young children hold on to a rope with knots spaced 2 feet apart?

- Allowing extra time and space for children to put on jackets and sweaters prior to getting into line?

- Complimenting those students who are maintaining order?

PERCEPTION OF TOUCH

Hypersensitivity to touch can make inadvertent human contact painful and disturbing. Inadvertent physical contact may provoke disruptive behavior in some children.

- Having the child who has a tendency to be disruptive go first or last in line? This will minimize possible tactile contact.

- Minimizing time expected to stand and wait in line?

- Allowing a child with suspected hypersensitivity to touch to wear a sweater or jacket indoors?

Organizing Behavior During Motor Time

Problems In This Area Could Be Related To:

DEGREE OF STRUCTURE

Inadequate structure may contribute to a sense of chaos during motor activities.

Have you tried • • •

- Reviewing how to play the game before actually playing it? Demonstrate verbally as well as visually.

- Implementing motor time in the classroom rather than outside? There are fewer distractions inside and students are more likely to follow classroom rules.

- Designating a boundary or place marker for each child? Try using carpet squares, chalk marks, or masking tape.

- Marking the boundaries of the game? For example, rope, yarn, masking tape, or chalk can be used to mark a game circle, or start and finish lines.

- Using signals for control? Two blows of a whistle to signal freeze. Practice *Simon Says* or freeze-type games.

- Stopping action between turns in order to get everyone's attention and therefore regain control?

- Giving one direction at a time? For example: "Stand on the line." PAUSE. Wait until the class is on the line. "We are going to . . . " (one direction). PAUSE. "and . . ." (a second direction).

- Scheduling and implementing frequent (daily) motor time so that students become familiar with behavioral expectations during motor activities?

- Working with small groups of children (approximately 6-8 in a group)? Divide the children by using a coding system (color, number, animal).

- Making a rule for how loose balls and scattered bean bags will be handled? Designate a person to collect these items so that the entire class does not lose time and organization.

- Scheduling a calming familiar backup game if the structure of a new game fails? Before a new game is discarded, try to alter the structure for future success.

Problems In This Area Could Be Related to:

Have you tried • • •

BROAD RANGE
OF SKILLS

Activities that are too easy
or too difficult tend to
elicit disruptive behavior.

- Initially having the entire class play a game at the lower skill level? Observe the more advanced students' sportsmanship, social communication, cooperation.

- Giving the students different assignments within the game? For example:
  Jump Rope — One child can be expected to jump the turning rope, while another proceeds to run through the turning rope.
  Target Games — The size and distance can be varied for each child.
  Throw and Catch Games — The students can be paired high skill with high skill or alternated high skill/low skill.

- Complimenting the children for cooperation? For example, compliment the student who is at the higher level. "I like the way you are helping Johnny." "You are doing a nice job working with Susie." At the same time, recognize the student at the lower level. "Nice try, John."

- Allowing a different number of turns for each child depending on skill level?

- Considering ways to make the game easier or more difficult prior to implementing the activity?

- Integrating children from other classrooms with similar skill levels?

- Dividing the class into several groups (one group for every available adult) to practice at various skill levels?

- Allowing a child who is having difficulty 10 to 15 minutes of extra practice time prior to classroom motor time? Try the "buddy system," working with a classmate who can assist with practice.

Problems In This Area Could Be Related To:

Have you tried • • •

BODY AWARENESS

Inaccurate awareness of where, how, and with what force body parts are moving in relation to objects can cause personal belongings to be disorganized.

- Stabilizing school supplies by weighting the child's pencil box and other containers? Use washers or plaster of paris.
- Triangular finger grips on pencils and crayons to prevent them from rolling off the desk?
- A clipboard and large bulldog clips to keep papers together?

VISUAL — SPATIAL PERCEPTION

Difficulty with figure-ground perception (identifying objects with a rival background) can contribute to a problem with sorting and organizing personal belongings.

- Keeping only necessary items on desk top?
- Allowing limited number of personal belongings at school?
- Designating a place or container for each belonging?
- Scheduling a set time each day to organize belongings?
- A color coded filing system? Folded construction paper of different colors can signify different subjects or complete and incomplete work.
- Discussing strategies for organizing personal belongings? Ideas include talking about sorting like objects, same and different characteristics of objects. This can be applied to cleaning a bedroom, doing the dishes, sorting collections of rocks, bugs, or sea shells, etc.

Problems In This Area Could Be Related To:

Have you tried • • •

BODY AWARENESS

Deficient strength and muscle tone in the muscles may make it tiring to sit erect for long periods. Work against resistance gives the muscles and joints better feedback about where the body is in relation to objects in the environment.

- Placing a heavy bean bag on a lap?

- Periodically giving firm hand pressure on the child's shoulders?

- Providing a brief time of classroom aerobics? Jumping, running in place, etc. may be the input the child needs to stay in his seat for longer periods of time.

- Alternating centers for work? Try providing a specific place to work where the child can stand, kneel, or lie prone. Expect at least five minute's work in each position.

- Bean bag chairs to aid in supporting body weight more comfortably?

- Expecting less erect posture, particularly during academic tasks requiring high concentration and towards the end of the day?

PERCEPTION OF TOUCH

A hypersensitivity to touch may make it difficult for some children to stay in their seat because they are trying to avoid inadvertent touch by the child next to them.

- Spacing children so that they are not sitting near enough to touch one another?

- Allowing the child to wear his favorite sweater or jacket when he is in situations where he will be near other children?

- Markers to help designate personal space when sitting on the floor?

Problems In This Area Could Be Related To:

Have you tried • • •

BODY AWARENESS

Poor automatic awareness of where, how, and with what force body parts are moving can account for torn, wrinkled work, holes in papers, and broken pencils.

- A tripod pencil grip? This may help a child who is tense relax his grip, enabling him to better control the amount of pressure he uses.

- Providing the child with thicker paper? Try gluing the child's writing paper onto construction paper for extra support?

- Playing pre-writing warm-up exercises or motor time games of wheelbarrow walking or tug-of-war? These games "wake up" some of the muscle groups used for good fine motor control.

- Pouring exercises? Child experiments with trying to pour from a cup or pitcher different amounts of sand, lentils, rice, or liquid. Strive for accuracy in force of movement.

- Bean bag games using bean bags of different weights and targets of varying distances? These games challenge the muscles to react to where, how, and with what force they are moving.

VISUAL — SPATIAL PERCEPTION

Inaccurate perception of the relationship of one's body to external space can contribute to a disorganized approach to a task. Faulty interpretation of the spatial relationships of objects, letters, and words to one another also contribute to messy work.

- Using quadrile paper for math? (see appendix)

- Emphasizing spatial terms? Use colored tape on desk. On left side use green to show starting point. On right side, red to show stopping point.

- Taping paper to desk at no more than a 45° angle?

- Art projects that require spatial precision?

- A shield or folding paper to eliminate visual distractions? Cut a hole in a piece of card stock paper the average size of a word or sentence. This can be placed over the paper a child is working on and moved when appropriate.

- Motor time activities that incorporate precision into movement? Games such as hop scotch challenge precision, accuracy, and neatness.

- A popsicle stick, tongue depressor, or strip of paper to mark a space between words? (see appendix)

- Pre-marked paper? Try premarking paper, indicating space appropriate for name, date, and subject. (see appendix)

Sportsmanship And Cooperation

Problems In This Area Could Be Related To:

Have you tried • • •

PEER INTERACTION

Poor peer interaction may interfere with good sportsmanship. The negative behavior of one or two students can spoil the fun of the activity.

- A review of the classroom rules? For example, "Do we have a rule about . . .?"

- Positive reinforcement techniques? Give immediate honest and positive comments on each small effort or appropriate social interaction. "I like how you are waiting for your turn." "That was nice of you to help Johnny."

- Ignoring disruptive behavior while complimenting desired behavior? "I like the way the red team is lining up. They can be first."

- Scheduling consistent motor time opportunities to practice sportsmanship?

- Providing game ideas for structured recess? Leisure time without a plan is a problem for some children.

- Structuring the game so that everyone wins and no one loses? Rules of most traditional games can be changed so that no one is eliminated.

- Changing roles frequently in games so that students can experience being leader vs. participant, first vs. last, etc.?

- Adding a cooperative component to "dodge ball" type games? For example, pass the ball three times before throwing it.

- Avoiding chase-type games?

- Providing enough equipment so that everyone can participate within a reasonable amount of time? Try to reduce time that children are waiting for a turn.

- Dividing teams in advance, or varying the method used for choosing sides? Avoid teams chosen by students, unless the method is objective.

PERCEPTION OF TOUCH

Hypersensitivity to touch can make inadvertent human contact painful or disturbing. Inadvertent physical contact may provoke disruptive behavior in some children.

- Allowing the child to wear his favorite sweater or jacket when he will be near other children?

- Markers to designate personal space?

- Talking about the game strategy to the child who is suspected of being hypersensitive to touch? If appropriate, mention that sometimes another child may accidentally bump into him, and not to worry.

- Allowing the hypersensitive child to have a larger personal space when participating in group activities?

Writing With Pencils

Problems In This Area Could Be Related To:

Have you tried • • •

FINE MOTOR CONTROL

A tool is only as accurate
as the hands and fingers
that control it.

- Hand grasp-strengthening activities? For example,
  holding on to the ropes of a swing, playing tug-of-war,
  using a hole punch, spraying with trigger-type spray
  bottles can help strengthen grasp.

- Kneading, poking, and rolling playdoughs and clays
  of various densities to develop basic hand and
  finger skill?

- Providing opportunities for the child to use a variety
  of tools? Try some of the suggestions in this manual
  for tool activities.

- Letting the child practice penmanship on the blackboard?

- Art projects requiring less precise use of pencils and
  crayons?

- Limiting the number of written assignments?

- Allowing typed reports, oral reports, or reports
  dictated onto a cassette?

- Using adult-sized pencils and crayons in kindergarten?
  Sometimes these are easier for little fingers to control.

- Wrapping a pencil with silly putty or playdough?
  This may help to relax a tense grip.

- Discussing the importance of neat penmanship?
  Sometimes messy handwriting is related to a
  poor attitude.

VISUAL — SPATIAL
PERCEPTION

OCULAR MOTOR
CONTROL

The correct interpretation
of the spatial relationship
of objects, letters, and words
to one another is essential to
legible writing.

Coordinated eye movements
are important for the eyes
to smoothly guide the hands.

- Practicing spatial relationships using manipulative
  toys to duplicate sequences or structures?

- Letter formation with finger paint? Try shaving
  cream on a desk.

- Practicing writing letters in the air with streamers?

- Writing letters with a paintbrush and water on
  the cement?

- Practicing letters with stencils?

- Taping the alphabet to the top of the desk for
  easy reference?

- Providing a marker to use between words as they
  are written to help the child with proper spacing?
  (see appendix)

- Playing balloon, suspended ball, and bean bag games
  during motor time? Some children need to be reminded
  to look at the object they are coordinating with
  their hand.

- Using smaller ruled paper? Sometimes it is easier
  to write smaller.

Ball And Balloon Games
Primary Sensory And Motor Components
Challenged In Each Activity

	AUDITORY PROCESSING	BODY AWARENESS	COORDINATING BODY SIDES	FINE MOTOR	MOTOR PLANNING	OCULAR CONTROL	PERCEPTION OF MOVEMENT	PERCEPTION OF TOUCH	VISUAL-SPATIAL PERCEPTION
Balloon Volley	x				x	x			
Bucket Ball		x							x
Bunt Baseball			x			x			x
Center Stride Ball					x		x		
Circle Relay	x	x							
Crab Walk Soccer					x	x	x		
Foot Volley					x		x		
Kanga Ball			x		x				x
Marble Ball					x	x			
Punch Ball					x				
Suspended Ball					x	x			
Target Soccer		x			x				

Balloon Volley

Equipment

Large round balloon — one per five to seven children.

Activity

A group of five to seven children form a circle. The children try to keep the balloon in the air for as long as possible by hitting it as directed. Try using two hands together, left hand, right knee, head, elbow, etc. To maintain order, have the child with the balloon hit it to a child that the teacher names. The children waiting are encouraged to watch the balloon. One child can stand in the center of the circle and volley the balloon to each consecutive child, who catches the balloon before returning it.

For variations, try volleying across a low volley-ball net, or try volleying with a two-handed bat. (see appendix)

This activity works better indoors.

Teacher Observations

Auditory Processing: Can the child follow the verbal command when given?

Motor Planning: Can the child anticipate and make appropriate changes in body position to hit the balloon?

Ocular Control: Can the child visually pursue the balloon?

31

Bucket Ball

Equipment

Tennis balls — one per child plus four extra balls. Large deep bucket or wastebasket.

Activity

The children form a large circle and the bucket is placed in the center. Each child is given a tennis ball. When a child's name is called, he tries to bounce the ball into the bucket. Each time he succeeds, he gets an additional chance. If the ball bounces out of the bucket, it is counted as a successful attempt, and the child continues to play. Once a child misses, another child's name is called, and that child takes a turn.

Teacher Observations

Body Awareness: Does the child use sufficient force to successfully bounce the ball into the basket?

Visual-Spatial Perception: Is the child able to bounce the ball to successfully get it in the bucket?

Bunt Baseball

Equipment

Two-handed bottle bat. (see appendix)
Nerf or other lightweight ball, 9" approximately.
Base markers — one per child.

Activity

This activity has been modified by grouping the players onto a pie-shaped field. The catcher, batter, and pitcher are aligned in the traditional manner. The remaining children stand behind a base marker in a semi-circle behind the pitcher. The child up to bat grasps the two-handed bat at each end and attempts to bunt the ball. After the ball is hit, the closest baseman catches or retrieves it and throws it to the pitcher. The ball is then thrown from one baseman to the next around the semi-circle and back to the pitcher. The batter's objective is to "run" all the bases and reach home before the ball has returned to the pitcher.

This activity can be varied by having the batter hop, jump, run backwards, etc. when rounding the bases. The basemen can vary how they pass the ball by throwing it two-handed, overhand, through the legs, or bouncing it. If the children have difficulty understanding the concept of the game, it may need to be simplified by practicing each step separately.

Teacher Observations

Coordinating Body Sides: Can the child coordinate both hands together when bunting with the bat?

Ocular Control: Does the child track the ball in flight and effectively position his body to catch it?

Visual-Spatial Perception: Is the child able to judge the direction and distance to the other child when throwing the ball?

Center Stride Ball

Equipment   Playground ball.

Activity   The children form a circle standing with their feet
                             apart. Their shoes should be touching those of the
                             child positioned next to them. Each child attempts
                             to roll the ball through the legs of another child, or
                             to block the ball using their hands as it is rolled
                             toward them. If the ball passes through a child's
                             legs, that child retrieves the ball and returns it to
                             play. The goal is to complete the game without
                             allowing the ball to go between their legs.

Teacher Observations

                             Motor Planning: Is the child able to effectively
                             direct the ball?

                             Is the child able to consistently block the shot?

                             Perception of Movement: Is the child able to
                             maintain his balance while bending and
                             changing his center of gravity?

Circle Relay

Equipment

Kickball.

Activity

The children stand in a circle, arms-width apart, facing their neighbor's back. A ball is given to one of the children who begins to pass it over his head, between his legs, to the child behind him. The ball continues to be passed around the circle in this manner.

To vary the activity, the teacher may designate a repeated pattern to follow as the ball is passed. For example, three children pass over their head, two pass between their knees, repeat.

Children may also face the center of the circle and pass the ball in a designated pattern. You may incorporate bouncing, catching, or dribbling.

Teacher Observations

Auditory Processing: Is the child able to follow the verbal direction?

Body Awareness: Is the child able to position himself so he can pass the ball to the child behind him?

Crab-Walk Soccer

Equipment

Ball — punch ball, beach ball, or playground ball. Masking tape or chalk line or boxes for goals.

Activity

Children divide equally into two teams. Goals are set up approximately ten feet apart. The children assume a "crab-walk" position and the ball is thrown into the center. Each side tries to get the ball to their goal by bumping it with their body or kicking it with their foot. Hands may not be used.

Teacher Observations

Motor Planning: Can the child move forward, backwards, and sideways?

Does the child easily change direction of movement?

Ocular Control: Does the child maintain visual contact with the ball?

Perception of Movement: Can the child maintain his balance while lifting a leg to kick without falling or putting his seat down?

Foot Volley

Equipment

Beach ball or punchball — one per four to six children.

Activity

The children sit in a circle and propel the ball from one to another by kicking it. When the ball goes out of the circle the child retrieving it must grasp it using his feet. Hands may not be used. To maintain order, have the child with the ball volley it to a child the teacher names.

For variation, switch from volleying to passing the ball around the circle with the feet, elbows, wrists or hands. Try combinations of elbow/knee or hand/foot, etc. for holding the ball.

Teacher Observations

Motor Planning: Can the child direct the flight of the ball with his feet?

Can the child assume the various positions to pass the ball using a combination of body parts?

Perception of Movement: Can the child sitting maintain his balance while kicking the ball?

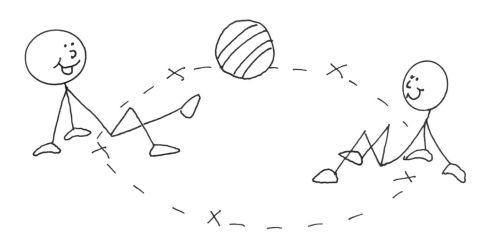

Kanga Ball

Equipment

Tennis balls or kick balls — one per three children.

Activity

Divide the children into groups of three. Two of the children sit ten to fifteen feet apart facing one another. The third child stands half way between the two children with his legs apart. The children who are seated are given a ball to roll back and forth between the middle child's legs. After six successful rolls, the children change places.

To vary this activity, the child in the middle may be asked to jump a half or whole turn over the ball as it rolls under his feet.

The number of children standing in the center can be varied. With each successful roll of the ball, another child can be added to straddle the center until as many children as possible stand in the center forming a tunnel for the ball.

Teacher Observations

Coordinating Body Sides: Is the child able to exert even pressure with both hands when pushing the ball?

Motor Planning: With each attempt, does the child learn to more accurately direct the ball?

Visual-Spatial: Does the child visually align the ball before rolling it?

Marble Ball

Equipment

Tennis balls — two per child.

Activity

The children sit on the floor and form a closed circle with their legs apart and feet touching. Each child is given one tennis ball. The remaining balls are placed in the center of the circle. When his name is called, the child rolls a tennis ball towards the cluster of tennis balls in the center of the circle, causing them to scatter. The object of the game is to hit the tennis balls in the center of the circle, similar to playing "marbles." The children may keep any of the tennis balls that come within arms reach. The tennis balls may be redistributed as needed.

To vary the activity, have two children roll their tennis balls across to one another without hitting any of the balls in the middle of the circle.

For another variation, have the children take turns trying to make two balls collide.

Teacher Observations

Motor Planning: Is the child able to accurately direct the roll of the tennis ball?

Ocular Control: Does the child sustain visual contact with the target as he rolls the ball?

Punch Ball

Equipment

Playground ball.

Activity

Children scatter to form an outfield with one child in the batter's position. No bases or pitcher are needed. The batter must bounce the ball and then hit it with both hands held together. The outfielder who catches the ball then changes places with the batter.

To increase the challenge, have the batter designate in what direction the ball will be hit.

Teacher Observation

Motor Planning: Can the child bounce the ball and successfully time the hit?

Can the child control the direction the ball is hit?

Suspended Ball

Equipment

Suspended ball or balloon — one per two to four children.
Two-handed bottle bat — one per suspended ball. (see appendix)
Targets — stickers, colored shapes, letters, numerals.

Activity

The ball is suspended at the child's shoulder level. The child sits, lies, kneels, or stands and hits the ball with his hands, finger, elbow, knee, or head. To easily accommodate hitting the ball from different positions, have stations with ball suspended at various heights.

Swing the ball to the child and have him catch it with his right hand, left hand, or with both hands on command. The child can hit the suspended ball with a two-handed bottle, paper towel, or wrapping paper roll.

Targets can be placed on the suspended ball. The child is asked to look at and hit the target as the ball moves.

Have the child throw bean bags at the suspended ball.

Teacher Observations

Motor Planning: Does the child anticipate and make appropriate changes in body position to hit the target?

Ocular Control: Can the child visually track the moving ball?

Target Soccer

Equipment

Soft playground ball.
Three weighted pop bottles. (see appendix)
One 2' X 4' target area — taped off.

Activity

The three pop bottles are evenly spaced two feet behind the target area. The children line up approximately fifteen feet from the center of the target area. One child plays the goalie. The goalie stands in the target area and stops the ball from hitting any of the bottles. He may not step outside the taped boundary or use his hands.

Teacher Observations

Body Awareness: Does the child use an appropriate amount of force to propel the ball?

Motor Planning: Is the child able to time his kick accurately?

Bean Bag Games
Primary Sensory And Motor Components
Challenged In Each Activity

	AUDITORY PROCESSING	BODY AWARENESS	COORDINATING BODY SIDES	FINE MOTOR	MOTOR PLANNING	OCULAR CONTROL	PERCEPTION OF MOVEMENT	PERCEPTION OF TOUCH	VISUAL-SPATIAL PERCEPTION
Animal Walk Bowling		X			X	X			
Bean Bag Balance					X		X		
Bean Bag Catch					X	X			
Bean Bags In A Basket	X	X							
Bean Bag Pass			X		X				
Bean Bag Sequence	X				X				
Bean Bag Target		X			X				X
Toss Across		X							X
Toss At A Rolling Ball					X	X			
Toss At A Target		X				X			
Toss, Jump, Pick-Up							X		X
Toss to Another						X	X		
Turtle Races		X						X	

Animal Walk Bowling

Equipment

Bean bags — one per team.
Weighted plastic pop bottle — one per three to four children. (see appendix)
Start and throw lines, 12-15 feet apart, of masking tape.

Activity

Groups of two to three children line up relay style on the starting line. The first child in each line animal walks to the throwing line where he picks up a bean bag and throws it at the weighted plastic pop bottles, attempting to knock them over. He then animal walks back to his team and goes to the end of the line. The teacher or a designated child sets up the pop bottles and returns the bean bags to the throwing line.

Have the children animal walk backward, sideways, and diagonally to add to the motor challenge for a variation.

Teacher Observations

Body Awareness: Can the child maintain the animal walk position while moving?

Motor Planning: Can the child assume the animal walk positions and sequence the steps required?

Ocular Control: Does the child make visual contact with the target while throwing?

Bean Bag Balance

Equipment

One bean bag per two children.
Start and finish lines, 12-14 feet apart, of
masking tape or chalk.

Activity

Groups of two to three children line up relay
style on the starting line. The first child in
each group assumes an animal walk posture
and balances a bean bag on a designated part
of his body. He then attempts to carry the
bean bag without dropping it as he animal
walks to the finish line. Should he drop the
bean bag, he must start over. If he drops it a
second time, he repositions the bean bag and
continues to the finish line. Once the child
reaches the finish line, he throws the bean
bag to the next child on his team who is
waiting on the starting line.

The weight and size of the bean bags may be
varied. A heavier bean bag may be easier
to balance.

Teacher Observations

Motor Planning: Can the child perform the
designated variety of movements?

Perception of Movement: Does the child
make adequate postural adjustments to
balance the bean bag?

Bean Bag Catch

Equipment

Bean bags — one per child.

Activity

Throw a bean bag up in the air and catch it when it comes down.

Throw a bean bag up in the air and clap a rhythm pattern with your hands. TOSS, CLAP, CLAP, CATCH.

Throw two bean bags up in the air, one in each hand, and catch the bean bags with the same hand.

Throw two bean bags up in the air and catch them with the opposite hands. Catch the bean bag thrown with the right hand in the left hand, and catch the bean bag thrown with the left hand with the right hand.

Throw a bean bag up in the air and try to touch it with your right or left foot.

Throw a bean bag up in the air. On command, catch the bean bag with the right hand, left hand, or both hands.

Throw bean bags in rhythmic sequences that include left, right, and both hands. For example: LEFT HAND — TOSS AND CATCH 2 TIMES. BOTH — TOSS AND CATCH ONE TIME. RIGHT HAND — TOSS AND CATCH 2 TIMES. REPEAT.

Keep two bean bags in motion by throwing one up in the air, watching it reach the top of its trajectory, then throwing the other one up, and so on.

Throw a bean bag up in the air and try to catch it with eyes closed. This activity requires the child to visualize the path that the bean bag will follow in its descent; and to predict where it will fall.

Teacher Observations

Motor Planning: Does the child move his body to catch the bean bag?

Ocular Control: Does the child sustain visual fixation on the bean bag while catching it?

Bean Bags In a Basket

Equipment

Bean bag — one per child.
Containers of varying diameters or baskets.

Activity

Children form a large circle around one or more containers. Each child holds a bean bag and progresses around a circle by walking, knee walking, jumping, hopping, skipping, etc. On command, the children stop. Each child takes his turn throwing the bean bag in the basket as directed. For example: The bean bags can be tossed underhand, overhand, under the leg, between the legs, over the shoulder, etc. When all the bean bags have been thrown, one child is delegated to collect and redistribute them.

This activity can be made more challenging by varying the diameter of the container, the height of the container, and/or the distance from the container.

Teacher Observations

Auditory Processing: Can the child control the impulse to throw the bean bag until his name is called?

Body Awareness: Is the child able to adjust the intensity of his throwing to compensate for changes in distance?

Bean Bag Pass

Equipment

Large bean bags — one per four to six children.
(see appendix)

Activity

Children sit or stand in a circle and pass a bean bag around the circle in a specified manner. They can pass using both hands together or pass the bean bag from one hand to the other hand. Try passing overhead, through legs, in back of body, crossing hands, around body, etc.

For older children who may enjoy a more competitive game of *Bean Bag Pass*, try *Relay Races* or *Hot Potato*.

Relay Races — Have the children form two lines and pass the desired number of bean bags in any designated manner.

Hot Potato — Have the children stand or sit in a circle and pass the bean bag "hot potato" around the circle while music plays. When the music stops, whoever is holding the bean bag must go to the center of the circle and jog or jump in place to the count of ten.

The weight of the bean bag can be varied for larger or smaller children.

Teacher Observations

Coordinating Body Sides: Is the child able to cross the midline of his body when passing the bean bag?

Motor Planning: Can the child pass a bean bag in the designated manner?

Bean Bag Sequence

Equipment

Bean bags — one per child.
Weighted plastic pop bottles — one per child.
(see appendix)
Start and throw lines, 12-15 feet apart, of
masking tape.

Activity

The children line up along the starting line. One
bean bag is placed in front of each child on the
throwing line and a weighted plastic pop bottle
is positioned five feet further from each bean
bag. The teacher chooses a sequence of motor
actions for each child, such as hop on one foot
two times, take a giant step and jump one time.
The child performs his sequence of motor actions
as he moves towards the throwing line. He then
picks up a bean bag, throws it at the bottles, and
walks back to the starting line. The teacher names
one of the children to reposition the bottles and
bean bags.

Teacher Observations

Auditory Processing: Does the child attend to
and follow the directions?

Motor Planning: Can the child sequence the
motor actions?

Bean Bag Target

Equipment

Bean bags — one per child.
Weighted plastic pop bottle — one per two children.
Parallel lines, 12-15 feet apart, of masking tape.

Activity

The children divide into pairs and line up facing each other on the lines. A bottle is placed in the center between each pair of children. Each child is given a colored bean bag as one or two colors are called. The children with those colors throw their bean bag at the target. The children throw their bean bags in a designated manner, such as underhand, overhand, under one knee, through a bent elbow, etc.

Teacher Observations

Body Awareness: Does the child attempt to control the thrust of his throw in order to hit the target?

Motor Planning: Can the child motor plan the position from which to throw the bean bag?

Visual-Spatial Perception: Is child successful in correcting inaccurate throws?

Toss Across

Equipment

Bean bags — one per two children.

Activity

Divide the class into two groups. Have the groups stand approximately twenty feet apart, one group facing the other. Have the children take turns throwing a bean bag to their partner. If the partner misses the bean bag, he must take a step closer. The object of the game is to catch the bean bag each time so that the child does not have to advance forward. This can be played in reverse, stepping back each time one of the children catches the bean bag.

As the children become more familiar with the rules, more than one child may throw at a time. For example: all of the children with a specific colored bean bag can throw simultaneously. This activity can also be varied by throwing while lying on the stomach, half-kneeling, kneeling, or squatting.

Teacher Observations

Body Awareness: Is child able to control the force and distance of his throw?

Visual-Spatial Perception: Is the child successful at correcting inaccurate throws?

Toss At a Rolling Ball

Equipment

Bean bags — one per child.
Playground ball.
Parallel lines, 10-12 feet apart, of masking tape or yarn.

Activity

The children are divided into two groups and seated facing each other on the lines. One child is selected to help the teacher roll the ball between the two rows of children. Each child is given a bean bag to throw at the ball as it is rolled back and forth.

To add an extra motor component, have the children half-kneel, stand on one foot, lie on their stomachs, or assume a crawling position while throwing.

Teacher Observations

Motor Planning: Is the child able to time the throw to hit the ball when it passes in front of him?

Ocular Control: Can the child visually track the moving target?

Toss At a Target

Equipment

Bean bags of various sizes and weights. Targets: plastic bottles, plastic bowling pins, hula hoops, laundry baskets, boxes, wastebaskets, buckets, coffee cans, lines made of masking tape, etc.

Activity

Bean bags can be thrown using a variety of throwing techniques, body postures, and throwing styles. The distance of the line or target can be varied to change the motor challenge.

Throw the bean bags over a line using a variety of throwing techniques such as overhand, underhand, with right hand, with left hand, with both hands.

Throw the bean bags over a line using various body postures such as kneeling, half-kneeling, on hands and knees, side-lying, etc. In addition, vary the throwing techniques.

Throw the bean bags at or into a target using various throwing styles such as over the shoulder, under one leg, between both legs, etc.

Throw the bean bags at a target while going down a playground slide.

Teacher Observations

Body Awareness: Does the child adjust the force of his throw when the weight of the bean bag or the distance of the target is changed?

Ocular Control: Does the child look at the target when he throws the bean bag?

Toss, Jump, Pick Up

Equipment

Large bean bag — one per child.
Start and finish lines, 12-15 feet apart,
of masking tape. (see appendix)

Activity

The children line up on the starting line.
When his name is called, each child tosses
his bean bag forward. Without taking extra
steps the child then jumps over the bean bag,
reaches down, picks it up, and throws it again
to repeat the sequence. A child must start
over if he throws the bean bag too far to
successfully jump over it, takes extra steps,
or loses his balance. The children repeat this
sequence until they reach the finish line.

Teacher Observations

Perception of Movement: Can the child jump
and maintain foot placement without losing
his balance?

Visual-Spatial Perception: Can the child judge
the approximate distance he can jump and then
throw the bean bag the correct distance?

54

Toss to Another

Equipment

Bean bags — one per two children.

Activity

Throw bean bag overhand or underhand with both hands.

Throw bean bag overhand or underhand to another person, varying the distance by stepping backward or forward.

Step forward and at the same time throw bean bag with the right or left hand. For example, step with the right foot and toss with the right hand. Try various combinations: left foot/left hand, right foot/left hand, left foot/right hand.

Throw the bean bag sidearm with both hands.

Throw the bean bag back and forth underhand/overhand, using the right hand and arm only.

Throw the bean bag back and forth underhand/overhand, using the left hand and arm only.

Give each child a bean bag. Throw the bean bag with the right hand and simultaneously catch one with the left hand. Throw the bean bag with the left hand and simultaneously catch one with the right hand.

Teacher Observations

Ocular Control: Does the child turn his head or close his eyes when the bean bag approaches his face? Does the child sustain visual fixation on the bean bag while catching it?

Perception of Movement: Does the child adjust his body to catch and throw the bean bag?

Turtle Races

Equipment

Turtle shells of large bean bags and/or jackets, blankets, throw rugs.
Start and finish lines, 12-15 feet apart, of masking tape or yarn.

Activity

The children line up at the starting line, forming teams for relays. Blankets, jackets, or rugs are placed on a child's back for his shell. The child crawls to the finish line, trying not to lose his shell.

To vary this activity, place objects on the stomach while in crab-walk position for a hermit crab race.

Teacher Observations

Body Awareness: Is the child able to maintain the posture with the addition of the bean bag, blanket, throw rug, etc.?

Perception of Touch: Does the child tolerate the texture or feel of his shell?

Games With Easily Made Equipment
Primary Sensory And Motor Components
Challenged In Each Activity

	AUDITORY PROCESSING	BODY AWARENESS	COORDINATING BODY SIDES	FINE MOTOR	MOTOR PLANNING	OCULAR CONTROL	PERCEPTION OF MOVEMENT	PERCEPTION OF TOUCH	VISUAL-SPATIAL PERCEPTION
A-Tisket, A-Tasket	X				X				
Catch Ball In A Cup					X	X			
Catch With A Scoop		X	X		X				
Circle Bunt Ball			X		X	X	X		
Cookie Baking			X					X	
Don't Spill the Cargo		X					X		
Dress-Up Relay				X	X			X	
Feed the Elephant				X					X
Hopscotch							X		X
Lummi Sticks	X		X		X				
Musical Chairs	X				X				
Pass It On								X	X
Pop Goes The Weasel			X				X		
Popcorn Popper	X				X				
Streamers			X		X				
Textured Finger Paints		X						X	
Touch And Tell								X	
Who Stole the Cookie	X		X		X				
Wiffle Ball Catch					X	X			
Yarn Packages			X		X		X	X	

A-Tisket, A-Tasket

Equipment

Handkerchief, Kleenex, or bean bag.

Activity

The children sit in a circle (use floor markers if needed). One child is chosen to be "It" and stands outside the circle holding a handkerchief. As the children sing (see music in appendix), "It" skips, or animal walks around the outside of the circle. During the words "I dropped it," "It" drops the handkerchief behind any child he chooses. He then continues around the circle back to the empty space. The new child becomes "It"—picks up the handkerchief, and chooses a new pattern of movement. Children can progress around the circle in opposite directions to avoid racing.

Song: A tisket, a tasket,
A green and yellow basket,
I wrote a letter to my love
And on the way I *dropped it.*
I dropped it, I dropped it,
And on my way *I dropped it*
A little boy (girl) picked it up
And put it in his (her) pocket.

This activity can be varied by having each child hold a bleach bottle scoop behind his back. (see appendix) The child who is "It" drops a bean bag into the bleach bottle scoop of any child he chooses. The new child then progresses around the circle, carrying the bean bag in his scoop.

Teacher Observations

Auditory Processing: Does the child follow through with appropriate timing to the directions of the song?

Motor Planning: Can the child execute various patterns of movement? Can the child follow the correct sequence and direction of play?

58

Catch Ball In a Cup

Equipment

Ping-pong or tennis ball — one per child.
Plastic cups — one per child.

Activity

Children stand arms-width apart in a line. Each child is given a cup in one hand and a ball in the other hand. The child bounces and catches his own ball as directed by the teacher. For example: "Everyone bounce the ball on the count of three and catch it."

To reduce distraction, children may take their turn when their name or number is called. Allow plenty of time for experimentation.

The motor demands of this activity can be increased by throwing and catching with a partner.

Teacher Observations

Motor Planning: Is the child able to time hand movements in order to catch the ball?

Ocular Control: Can the child maintain visual contact with the ball? Or does he tend to focus on the cup?

Catch With a Scoop

Equipment

Bean bags — one per two children.
Beach bottle scoops — one per two children.
(see appendix)
Start and finish lines made of masking tape
or chalk.

Activity

Children pair off, one with a scoop on the
starting line, one with a bean bag on the finish
line. The child with the bean bag throws the
bean bag to the child with the scoop. If the
child catches the bean bag he may take one
step forward. The child with the scoop then
tries to toss the bean bag. When the children
meet, they exchange equipment and repeat the
process, stepping back one step after each catch.

If there is a sufficient number of scoops, both
children may use them; this is a more difficult
task.

A timing sequence may be added. For example,
have the children count to a designated number
and toss the bean bag. The children can be cued
to throw the bean bag by stopping and starting a record.

Teacher Observations

Body Awareness: Does the child move arms
and body to reach out to catch the bean bag?

Coordinating Body Sides: Is the child able to
throw the bean bag using the scoop?

Motor Planning: Does the child maintain
an upward tilt to the scoop so that the bean
bag will not fall out?

Circle Bunt Ball

Equipment

Two-handed bottle bat — one per child.
(see appendix)
Tennis ball.

Activity

Children form a circle and lie on their stomachs facing each other. Each child holds the bat with two hands and bunts the ball across the circle. The object is to keep the ball rolling and inside the circle.

To avoid fatigue, allow the child to use one hand on the bat or change to the kneeling position. This activity can also work well in small groups or pairs.

Teacher Observations

Coordinating Body Sides: Can the child keep both hands on the bat to hit the ball, or does he try to let go with one hand?

Motor Planning: Can the child time his movements in order to make contact with the ball?

Ocular Control: Does the child follow movements of the ball with his eyes?

Perception of Movement: Is the child able to hold his head and upper trunk up against gravity, thereby freeing arms to use the bat?

Cookie Baking

Equipment

Two-handed bottle bat — one per two
children. (see appendix)

Activity

Divide children into pairs. One child becomes
the "cookie dough" and lies flat on his stomach.
The baker "rolls" out the dough, using the
two-handed bat as a rolling pin. Roll each
arm, leg, and the back with firm pressure.
When rolling is finished, the baker can draw
a shape on the back to decorate the cookie.
The child who is the dough tries to guess what
shape was drawn. The children then trade
positions.

Some children may not tolerate having
another child "roll" them, but may accept
this activity if they are able to "roll"
themselves.

Teacher Observations

Coordinating Body Sides: Can the child
smoothly roll the bat using both hands?

Perception of Touch: Does the child on the
floor tolerate both the firm pressure of the
rolling and the light pressure of a finger
drawing on the back?

Don't Spill the Cargo

Equipment

Container— saucepan, tray, plastic cup, spoons, or measuring cups.
Objects to be transported — cotton balls or lentils, popcorn, rice, or water.

Activity

Children are divided into groups of approximately four to six children. An equal number of children are to form a line approximately ten feet apart, opposite one another. A spillable object is transported from a child at the starting line to another child at the finish line. The object is relayed until each child has had a turn. The class attempts to cooperate by successfully transporting as much of the object as possible.

After each child has had a turn, the class combines the material and measures or counts the remaining material. The class works together to try to improve the amount transported and the time it takes for the class to finish.

Teacher Observations

Body Awareness: Does the child realize when the container is tipped?

Perception of Movement: Does the child make appropriate body adjustments to avoid tipping the container?

Dress-Up Relay

Equipment

Clothing — large shirts, coats, sweaters, pants, shorts, knee socks, mittens.
Two parallel lines made of masking tape or chalk, 10-12 feet apart.

Activity

Children line up on the first line. The teacher puts an item of clothing directly across from each child on the second line. The children are asked to knee walk, hop, skip, jump, or animal walk to their place of clothing and put it on. After dressing, each child progresses in the designated manner back to the first line.

This activity can be varied by having pairs of children sit opposite each other on the line. Each child is given an article of clothing to wear. Once they are dressed, the pairs progress to the center, exchange clothing , and return to their line. By eliminating buttons, cutting off sleeves, or using oversized clothing, this task can be gradated to various skill levels.

Teacher Observations

Fine Motor: Does the child have difficulty with fastenings?

Motor Planning: Is the child able to put on the piece of clothing correctly?

Perception of Touch: Does the child object to various textures of clothing?

Feed the Elephant

Equipment

Cylinders made of rolled gray construction paper fastened with paper clips — one per four children.

Activity

Children wad paper into small balls to form peanuts. Place the elephant's trunk (cylinder) on its side or on end. The children lie on their stomachs, trying to flip the paper peanut into the elephant's trunk.

To avoid fatigue, children may change position to hands and knees or kneeling. To increase difficulty of game, vary distance of elephant's trunk from child.

Teacher Observations

Fine Motor: Does the child have the dexterity to flip the paper peanut?

Visual-Spatial Perception: Can the child alter the force of his flip to improve target accuracy?

Hopscotch

Equipment

Chalk or tape.
Lagger (e.g., flat stone or bean bag).

Activity

Make a hopscotch court using chalk or tape, numbering each of the boxes. Four to six children can participate per court. Court formation can be varied to meet the skill level of the classroom (see below). Each player has a lagger. The first player tosses his lagger into box number one. That player must hop over the box and land into the next box on one foot without stepping on or over the line. The child continues on to the end.

The general rule is to hop on one foot in the single boxes and on two feet in the double boxes. In the last box the child jumps, making a half turn, and proceeds back to his lagger. He then picks it up without falling and continues out of the court. The process is repeated until the bean bag is thrown to the last box.

This activity may be modified to meet the individual child's skill level. Some children may need to jump with two feet instead of hopping or may perform better with a reduced number of boxes. Rules regarding stepping on the line may be eliminated. Children may be given several chances to set the lagger in the correct box.

Teacher Observations

Perception of Movement: Can the child jump and maintain foot placement without losing his balance?

Visual-Spatial Awareness: Can the child judge the approximate distance he can jump or throw to avoid touching the line?

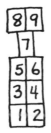 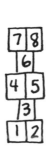 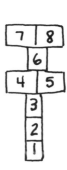

Lummi Sticks

Equipment

One set of lummi sticks per child. (see appendix)
Music — simple songs.

Activity

Lummi sticks are rhythm sticks. They are used to tap to a rhythm of a familiar rhyme or song.

Variations include combinations of tapping sticks together. Try tapping a body part, tapping the floor, tapping the ends of the sticks, tapping high, tapping low, tapping to the right, tapping to the left, or tapping under a raised knee. Let your music suggest your movements.

Teacher Observations

Coordination of Body Sides: Can the child simultaneously tap the sticks?

Auditory Processing: Does the child tap at the correct auditory cue?

Motor Planning: Is the child able to sequence several combinations of tapping movements?

Musical Chairs

Equipment

Carpet squares, music bean bags or boxes — one per child.

Activity

The game is played using bean bags, carpet squares, or boxes in place of chairs. The children walk around the circle. The game is played much like traditional musical chairs, however, no one is eliminated.

When the music stops, each child must stand on a bean bag, sit on a carpet square, or crawl into a box. The mode of locomotion may be varied each time. Try knee walking, walking backwards, crawling, and animal walks.

For older children, designate one bean bag, carpet square, etc., as the winner's spot. That person then chooses the next mode of locomotion.

Teacher Observations

Auditory Processing: Does the child respond quickly to musical cues? Does the child retain the game concept?

Motor Planning: Is the child able to perform the various modes of movement?

Pass It On

Equipment

Pencil.
Paper.

Activity

Children are divided into groups and are seated train style, facing one another's back. The last child in the line draws a letter, number, or shape on the person's back directly in front of him. The child who has the design drawn on his back, draws what he experiences on the back of the child in front of him. This is repeated until the first child in line receives the tactile message. He then draws on a paper or blackboard what was felt. The last child in line verifies the correctness of the message.

The order of the children may be rotated to facilitate the accuracy of the message.

To vary level of difficulty, try rhythmical tapping on one another's back or using consecutive letters to convey simple words or messages.

Teacher Observations

Perception of Touch: Does the child complain of unusual tickling or pain when the message is drawn?

Visual-Spatial Perception: Is the child able to duplicate design accurately?

Pop Goes the Weasel

Equipment

Weighted plastic pop bottles — one per three children. (see appendix)

Activity

Children sit in a circle, passing the bottles while singing *Pop Goes the Weasel* (see music in appendix). They must pass the bottles quietly. When "pop goes the weasel" is sung, all those with bottles shake them. Bottles can be passed in a variety of ways, behind the back, overhead, under the legs, etc.

Song: All around the mulberry bush
The monkey chased the weasel.
The weasel thought it was all fun
Pop! goes the weasel.

Teacher Observations

Coordinating Body Sides: Can the child easily cross the body's midline when passing the bottle?

Perception of Movement: Can the child control his movements so that the beans cannot be heard during the beginning of the song?

Popcorn Popper

Equipment

Weighted plastic pop bottles — one per four to six children. (see appendix)

Activity

Children sit in a circle. The weighted plastic pop bottle is passed around the circle in a designated manner. For example, the bottle can be passed with two hands, around the back, overhead, etc. The children chant *The Popcorn Popper Goes Pop.*

The object of the game is to pass the bottle very quietly until they hear the word "Pop." Each time the word "Pop" is sung, the children shake the bottle making a popping noise.

Chant:

> The popcorn popper goes POP!
> The popcorn popper goes POP!
> The popcorn popper goes POP, POP, POP!
> The popcorn popper goes POP!

Teacher Observations

Auditory Processing: Is the child able to sequence the correct number of "pops"?

Motor Planning: Is the child able to pass the weighted plastic pop bottle in the designated manner?

Streamers

Equipment
Streamers — two per child. (see appendix)

Activity
Children imitate the leader by forming circles, figure eights, letters, and numbers, etc., using whole arm movements. This may be done to music once the children have had some practice.

A different color streamer for each hand may be useful in teaching left/right discrimination.

Teacher Observations

Coordinating Body Sides: Can the child coordinate both hands together when performing mirror (same) movements and opposite movements?

Does the child turn his whole body to avoid crossing the midline?

Motor Planning: Does the child need to watch arms in order to execute motor patterns?

Textured Finger Paints

Equipment

Butcher or finger painting paper.
Finger paints.
Textures — sand, seeds (poppy, sesame, celery, bird, sunflower), rice, uncooked hot cereals, lentils, fine macaroni, Ivory Snow Flakes.
Tape.
Newsprint.

Activity

Cover the table top with butcher paper and secure the ends with tape. The teacher gives each child some finger paint and lets the child choose a variety of textures. Once the child has made a design, a print can be made by pressing newsprint or other plain paper over it.

Seasonal pictures can be made by whipping equal parts of Ivory Snow Flakes and water to make ghosts, snowmen, bunnies, and ducks.

Try finger painting gently over macaroni, rice, lentils, etc. that have been glued onto the paper.

Teacher Observations

Body Awareness: Is child able to keep the paint confined to the appropriate space, or does he unknowingly get paint all over himself?

Perception of Touch: Is child uncomfortable getting his hands into the different textures?

Touch and Tell

Equipment

Paper or cloth bag.
Small common objects.

Activity

Fill the bag with common objects. Seat the children in a circle on the floor. The teacher asks the child to feel for a specific object in the bag. The child removes it from the bag to see if he is correct. The object is then returned to the bag and the bag is passed to the next child.

This activity can be varied by giving each child an identical bag. The teacher or one child reaches inand removes one object. The other children see how quickly they can find a matching object.

Teacher Observations

Perception of Touch: Can the child find the common object by touch within a reasonable amount of time?

Is the child able to control the impulse to feel or to look at the object before identifying it?

Who Stole the Cookie

Equipment

Blank cards made of paper or cardboard, 3" X 3" — one per child.

Activity

Children sit tailor-fashion on the floor in a circle. The teacher gives each child a card face down. One of these has previously been designated as the cookie. While children chant, they keep beat by clapping, tapping, or other rhythmical body movements.

Group:
"Who stole the cookie from the cookie jar?"
"_____ (name of child) stole the cookie from the cookie jar."

Child:
"Who, me?"

Group:
"Yes, you!"

(Child named turns over his card and responds)

Child:
"Not me," or "Yes, me."

Group:
"Then who?"

If the child named did not have the cookie, then he chooses the next child and the sequence is repeated.

This game can be integrated into a reading or math lesson. Each child is given a card with a different spelling word or math problem. The teacher designates one card as the cookie. When a child's name is called, he turns over his card and spells the word or solves the problem to see if he has the cookie.

Teacher Observations

Auditory Processing: Can the child remember the chant and respond accordingly?

Coordinating Body Sides: Does the child have difficulty establishing or maintaining the rhythm?

Motor Planning: Is the child able to copy the movement patterns?

Wiffle Ball Catch

Equipment

Wiffle Ball catcher — one per child.
(see appendix)

Activity

Have the child try to catch the ball in the
scoop. See how many times the child can
catch the ball without missing. Try catching
on the count of three — "ONE, TWO, THREE,
CATCH!"

Teacher Observations

Motor Planning: Does the child have
difficulty "timing" the catch?

Ocular Control: Does the child keep his
eye on the ball?

Yarn Packages

Equipment

Thick yarn, 12-15 feet — one per two children.
Popsicle stick — one per two children.
Tape.

Activity

Have the children tape one end of the yarn to the stick and wrap the yarn around it. Children pair off and take turns wrapping the yarn around each other between the shoulders and knees. When the "package" has beenwrapped, the child turns his body to unwrap himself. As he turns, the child with the stick quickly winds the yarn back onto the stick. The children then change places.

For a variation, the child who is wrapped with yarn stands still while the other child unwraps the "package."

If the child finds it too stressful to have the yarn around his arms, then keep arms free.

Teacher Observations

Coordinating Body Sides: Can the child perform the bilateral task of wrapping the yarn around the stick?

Motor Planning: Can the child figure out which direction to turn his body in order to wind or unwind the yarn?

Perception of Movement: Does the child become dizzy easily during the activity?

Does the child continue to spin himself after he is unwrapped?

Can the child maintain balance while turning?

Perception of Touch: Does the child react negatively to the sensation of the yarn?

Games Without Equipment
Primary Sensory and Motor Components
Challenged In Each Activity

	AUDITORY PROCESSING	BODY AWARENESS	COORDINATING BODY SIDES	FINE MOTOR	MOTOR PLANNING	OCULAR CONTROL	PERCEPTION OF MOVEMENT	PERCEPTION OF TOUCH	VISUAL-SPATIAL PERCEPTION
Aerobic Stepping	X	X	X		X				
Animal Walks		X			X				
Charades			X		X				
Duck Duck Goose	X				X			X	
Hand Clapping			X		X				
Hokey Pokey	X	X					X		
Jimmy Crack Corn	X				X		X		
Johnny Pounds With One Hammer			X		X				
Lion Hunt		X			X				
London Bridge					X		X	X	
Melt The Ice		X			X				
Mirror Image		X			X	X			
Pretzel		X			X				
Progressive Aerobics	X		X		X		X		
Red Light, Green Light	X	X			X				
Red Rover					X		X		
Ring Around the Rosy	X	X					X		
Spinning Statue Freeze		X			X		X		
The Thousand Legged Worm	X	X			X		X		
The Tortoise And The Hare	X				X				
We Waded In The Water		X						X	

Aerobic Stepping

Equipment None.

Activity Children are continuously marching in place or in a circle while chanting:

Chant:
> Kick your knees up step in time
> Never need a reason
> Never need a rhyme
> Kick your knees up step in time.

With each round, change the activity slightly. For example:

- Swing your arms and step in time.
- Close your eyes and step in time.
- Step so soft (hard, fast, slow) and step in time.
- Circle your arms and step in time
- Touch your shoulders and step in time
- Clap your hands and step in time
- Kick your right leg and step in time.

Teacher Observations

Auditory Processing: Can the child process the words to the song and execute the correct movement?

Body Awareness: Can the child move his limbs without visually watching his movements?

Coordinating Body Sides: Does the child maintain a reciprocal stepping pattern, i.e., step with right foot then left foot?

Motor Planning: Does the child have difficulty stepping and doing arm or finger movements simultaneously?

Animal Walks

Equipment

None.

Activity

Animal walks can be practiced to music, used in place of running or walking in traditional children's games or used in relay races.

Teacher Observations

Body Awareness: Can the child make postural adjustments to assume positions and maintain the various positions?

Motor Planning: Can the child copy the designated animal walk without physical cues?

Bear

Assume creeping posture, progress forward and backwards, moving arms and legs of same side simultaneously. Keep the head down.

Bird

Stand on tiptoes and wave the arms slowly up and down. As the "wings" move faster, run tippy-toe around as if you were flying. As the flapping slows down the bird comes slowly to a stop.

Animal Walks
—Continued—

Bunny

Squat low on heels and place hands palm down on floor. Move the hands forward, and bring the feet forward between the hands with a little jump.

Crab

In a squatting position, reach backward with the arms and put both hands flat on the floor behind you. Raise up until the head, neck, and body are in a straight line. Walk or run in this inverted position.

Duck

Do a knee bend. Place your hands around your ankles. Walk forward one foot at a time, but remain in the knee-bent position.

Animal Walks
—Continued—

Elephant

Bending forward at the hips, allow the arms to hang limp. Big lumbering steps should sway you from side to side as you walk, imitating an elephant and his trunk.

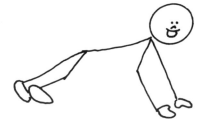 

Inchworm

Support the body by hands and toes, keeping body in a straight line. With hands remaining stationary, walk the feet towards the hands, taking tiny steps. Keep the legs straight. Next, keeping the feet stationary, walk the hands forward in tiny steps until the first position is reached.

Animal Walks
—Continued—

Horses Galloping

Gallop forward with hands held simulating grasp on reins. Change and lead off with opposite foot.

Horses Prancing

Stand straight, with hands held simulating grasp on reins. Lift knee high with toes pointed. Just as the foot touches the ground again, lift the other knee vigorously. Repeat in a rhythmical motion with forward momentum.

Animal Walks
—Continued—

Kangaroo

Stand with the feet together. Bend the elbows out from the body. Let the hands dangle limply. Bend the knees and jump forward.

Monkey

Run forward with both hands on the floor and the knees slightly bent.

Mule Kick

Drop to a squat position. Place the palms of the hands on the floor, between the knees. Bear weight on the hands and kick the feet backward vigorously. When the feet hit the ground, stand erect and take two steps forward. Repeat sequence.

Animal Walks
—Continued—

Rooster

Bending forward at the waist, grasp the ankles. Keep the knees as straight as you can. Walk forward.

Seal

Assume a prone position on the floor. Push the body up with extended arms. Walk forward with the arms while the feet drag behind.

Charades

Equipment

None.

Activity

The class is divided into groups of five to six children. The teacher quietly tells one child in the group his charade. The child communicates the charade to the other children by using appropriate body movements. The first child to raise his hand and correctly identify the action is next.

Charades can be played using a number of different themes. It can be structured from a simple one-step sequence to a more complex sequence of actions. Pictures or written cue cards may be used for variation.

Suggested Themes

Animals
  Elephant, donkey, rabbit, monkey, etc.
Emotions
  Angry, happy, embarrassed, confused, frightened, surprised, etc.
Sports
  Ice skating, skiing, soccer, hopscotch, roller skating, tennis, jump rope, archery, etc.
Familiar Tasks
  Brushing hair/teeth, getting dressed, making a bed, washing dishes, emptying the trash, etc.
Occupations
  Fireman, policeman, nurse, secretary, etc.

Teacher Observations

Body Awareness: Is the child able to coordinate his arms or legs in miming the charade? Or does he seem to lack awareness of what the body parts are doing?

Motor Planning: Is the child able to give appropriate gestures when interpreting his charade?

How complex are the child's ideas for gesturing?

Does he use a single movement or a sequence of movements to describe his charade?

Duck, Duck, Goose

Equipment   None.

Activity   The children sit in a circle or assume a designated posture. Carpet squares or place markers
may be used for each child, if needed. One child
is "it." He progresses around the outside of the
circle in a designated animal walk. As he passes
each child, he taps the child gently, saying
"duck" or "goose." If he says "goose," then the
child tapped pursues the child who was "it"
around the circle in the same designated
manner until the vacant space is reached.
The child tapped then becomes "it" and repeats
the process.

If the class becomes too chaotic during the
chase sequence, have the child who is tapped
go in the opposite direction to reach the
empty space.

Hoppity-hops may be used for older children.

Teacher Observations

Auditory Processing: Does the seated child
anticipate and respond to verbal cue of "goose"?

Motor Planning: Can the child copy the
designated animal walk without physical
cues?

Perception of Touch: Does the seated child
appear unaware of being touched or over-
sensitive to being touched when he is tapped?

Hand Clapping

The following clapping patterns are presented in a developmental sequence beginning with individual clapping patterns and progressing to clapping patterns with partners. They work well with almost any song and the timing can be altered to fit a particular rhythm. The most simple form of clapping is to repeat the same one-step pattern without crossing the midline of the body. Next in order of difficulty is to vary the clapping sequence, maintaining the same rhythm again without crossing the midline. Variations include assuming different body positions and clapping different body parts. Clapping variations which include crossing the body's midline are most difficult and are presented last.

One-Step Clapping Pattern

- Clap own hands to music or rhymes
- Slap own thighs (knees, shoulders, elbow)

Two-Step Sequence

- Clap own hands; slap own thighs
- Clap own hands; tap own shoulder
- Clap own hands; tap own head

Two-Step Sequence with Repetitive Action

- Clap own hands twice; slap thighs twice
- Clap own hands three times; slap thighs three times

Three Step Sequence

- Clap own hands once, slap thighs once, slap the floor once
- Clap own hands, slap backs of hands on thighs, slap the floor

Right and Left Hands Take Turns

- Clap; slap left hand on left thigh; clap; slap right hand on right thigh
- Clap; slap left hand on left thigh; slap right hand on right thigh; clap

Crossing the Midline of the Body

- Clap; cross arms and slap thighs
- Clap; slap left hand on right thigh; slap right hand on left thigh; clap

Partner Hand Clapping

- Clap own hands; slap partner's hands
- Clap own hands twice; slap partner's hands twice
- Clap own hands once; slap partner's hands; slap own thighs
- Clap; slap partner's left hand with own right hand; slap partner's
     right hand with own left hand
- Clap; slap partner's right hand with own right hand; slap partner's
     left hand with own left hand

Hand Clapping Rhymes

A Sailor Went to Sea
(see music in appendix)

A sailor went to sea, sea, sea,
To see what he could see, see, see,
But all that he could see, see
Was the bottom of the deep blue sea, sea, sea.

Bingo
(see music in appendix)

There was a farmer had a dog,
And BINGO was his name - O
B - I - N - G - O
B - I - N - G - O
B - I - N - G - O
And BINGO was his name - O.

Down By The Banks

Down by the banks of the Hanky Panky,
Where the bullfrogs jump from bank to banky,
With an eeps, ops, oops, ups,
He missed the lilly and he went ker-plop.

Hambone
(see music in appendix)

Hambone, Hambone, have you heard?
Papa's gonna buy me a mockingbird.

If that mockingbird don't sing
Papa's gonna buy me a diamond ring.

If that diamond ring don't shine
Papa's gonna buy me a fishing line.

Hambone, Hambone, where you been?
Around the world and I'm going again.

Hambone, Hambone, where's your wife?
In the kitchen cooking rice.

Hand Clapping Rhymes
– Continued –

Head and Shoulders
(see music in appendix)

Head and shoulders, Baby
One, two, three.
Head and shoulders, Baby
One, two, three.
Head and shoulders,
Head and shoulders,
Head and shoulders, Baby
One, two, three.

Knees and ankles, Baby
One, two, three.
Knees and ankles, Baby
One, two, three.
Knees and ankles
Knees and ankles
Knees and ankles, Baby
One, two, three.

Turn around, Baby

Touch the ground, Baby.

Head and Shoulders, Knees and Toes

Head and shoulders, knees and toes
Knees and toes.
Head and shoulders, knees and toes
Knees and toe-oe-oe-oes.
Eyes and ears and mouth and nose.
Head and shoulders, knees and toes
Knees and toes.

Hand Clapping Rhymes
– Continued –

Long Legged Sailor
(see music in appendix)

Have you ev-er, ev-er, ev-er in your long legged life,
Seen a long leg-ged sai-lor and his long leg-ged wife?

No, I've never, never, never in my long legged life,
Seen a long legged sailor and his long legged wife.

Miss Lucy Had a Baby
(see music in appendix)

Miss Lucy had a baby
She named it Tiny Tim
She put him in the bathtub
To see if he could swim.

He drank up all the water
He ate up all the soap
He tried to eat the bathtub
But it wouldn't go down his throat.

Miss Lucy called the Doctor
Miss Lucy called the Nurse
Miss Lucy called the lady
With the alligator purse.

Hand Clapping Rhymes
— Continued —

Miss Mary Mack
(see music in appendix)

Miss Mary Mack, Mack, Mack
All dressed in black, black, black
With silver buttons, buttons, buttons
All down her back, back, back.

She asked her mother, mother, mother
For fifteen cents, cents, cents
To see the elephant, elephant, elephant
Jump over the fence, fence, fence.

He jumped so high, high, high
He reached the sky, sky, sky
And didn't come back, back, back
Till the Fourth of July, ly, ly.

Peas Porridge Hot

Peas porridge hot
Peas porridge cold
Peas porridge in the pot
Nine days old.

Some like it hot
Some like it cold
Some like it in the pot
Nine days old.

Daddy likes it hot
Mommy likes it cold
I like it in the pot
Nine days old.

Hand Clapping Rhymes
– Continued –

Playmate
(see music in appendix)

Playmate
Come out and play with me
And bring your dol-lies three
Climb up my ap-ple tree
Look down my rain barrel
Slide down my cel-lar door
And we'll be jol-ly friends
For-ev-er more, more, more!

Pretty Little Dutch Girl
(see music in appendix)

I am a pret-ty lit-tle Dutch girl,
As pret-ty as pret-ty can be.
And all the boys in the neigh-bor-hood
Are cra-zy o-ver me.

My boyfriend's name is Mellow
He comes from the land of Jello
With pickles for his toes
And a cherry for his nose
And that's the way my story goes.

Skida Marink
(see music in appendix)

Skida marink a-dink a-dink,
Skida a-dink a-do.
I love you.

I love you in the morning,
And in the afternoon.
I love you in the evening,
And underneath the moon.

Oh skida marink a-dink a-dink,
Skida a-dink a-do.
I LOVE YOU.
I LOVE YOU!

Hand Clapping Rhymes
– Continued –

Ten Little Indians
(see music in appendix)

One little, two little, three little Indians.
Four little, five little, six little Indians.
Seven little, eight little, nine little Indians
Ten little Indian Boys.

Ten little, nine little, eight little Indians.
Seven little, six little, five little Indians.
Four little, three little, two little Indians.
One little Indian Boy.

The Bear Went Over The Mountain
(see music in appendix)

The bear went over the mountain,
The bear went over the mountain,
The bear went over the mountain
To see what he could see.
And all that he could see,
And all that he could see
Was the other side of the mountain,
The other side of the mountain
Was all that he could see!

The bear went over the river,
The bear went over the river,
The bear went over the river
To see what he could see.
And all that he could see,
And all that he could see
Was the other side of the river,
The other side of the river,
The other side of the river,
Was all that he could see!

This Old Man
(see music in appendix)

This old man he played ONE
He played knick-knack on his thumb
With a knick-knack patty wack
Give your dog a bone
This old man came rolling home.

This old man he played TWO
He played knick-knack on his shoe
With a knick-knack patty wack
Give your dog a bone
This old man came rolling home.

This old man, he played THREE
He played knick-knack on his knee.

This old man, he played FOUR
He played knick-knack on his door.

This old man, he played FIVE
He played knick-knack on his hive.

This old man, he played SIX
He played knick-knack on his sticks.

This old man, he played SEVEN
He played knick-knack up in heaven.

This old man, he played EIGHT
He played knick-knack on his gate.

This old man, he played NINE
He played knick-knack just in time.

This old man, he played TEN
He played knick-knack once again.

Hokey Pokey

Equipment

None.
(see music in appendix)

Activity

Children form a circle and follow the words of the song.

Stress only one body side throughout the activity to reinforce the concept of left or right. Vary the activity by performing it in standing, sitting, kneeling, and half-kneeling positions.

Song: You put your right hand in
You put your right hand out
You put your right hand in
And shake it all about.
You do the hokey-pokey
BEND ELBOWS, WIGGLE FINGERS UP, SWAY HIPS
And you turn yourself around
That's what it's all about!
CLAP IN RHYTHM

Verses:

- You put your right foot in . . .
- You put your right shoulder in . . .
- You put your right hip in . . .
- You put your head in . . .
- You put your whole self in . . .

Teacher Observations

Auditory Processing: Can the child imitate the words of the song?

Body Awareness: Can the child isolate the appropriate body part to move?

Perception of Movement: Can the child maintain orientation and place while turning? Can the child balance on one foot?

Jimmy Crack Corn

Equipment

None.
(see music in appendix)

Activity

Children form circle and follow the words of the song.

Song: Jimmy crack corn and I don't care
Jimmy crack corn and I don't care
Jimmy crack corn and I don't care
My master's gone away.

Jump up and down and I don't care
Jump up and down and I don't care
Jump up and down and I don't care
My master's gone away.

Verses:

- Hop on one foot and I don't care . . .
- Touch your toes and I don't care . . .
- Shake your hands and I don't care . . .
- Go in circles and I don't care : . .

Teacher Observations

Auditory Processing: Does the child quickly respond to new directions in the song or does he perseverate on the previous activity until he realizes that the other children are doing something different?

Motor Planning: Can the child use his body to imitate the words of the song?

Perception of Movement: Can the child balance on one foot, hop on one foot, go in circles without falling over?

Johnny Pounds With One Hammer

Equipment

None.
(see music in appendix)

Activity

Children sit on the floor in a line and duplicate the rhythm and motions of the leader. The leader sings:

Song: Johnny pounds with one hammer
One hammer, one hammer
Johnny pounds with one hammer
Now he pounds with two.
(Now he pounds with three.)

The leader pounds the floor with a fist. With each increase in number (one, two, three . . .), another part of the body is moved in unison to the beat. This continues until three or four body parts are "pounded" simultaneously. The tune ends with:

Johnny pounds with four hammers,
Now he is all through.

Keep this activity short because it can be fatiguing.

Teacher Observations

Coordinating Body Sides: Can the child maintain the rhythm of the activity?

Can the child continue to maintain the rhythm as additional body parts assume the motion of therhythm?

Motor Planning: Can the child direct his body to follow the leader?

98

Lion Hunt

Equipment

None.

Activity

Children mime movements as the teacher narrates the actions involved in catching a lion while on a safari. Begin the game, clapping in rhythm to the chant:

> Going on a lion hunt. (Clapping)
> Going to catch a big one. (Clapping)
> STOP. (Stop)
>
> I see a dark marshy jungle! (Hand over brow to imitate looking ahead.)
> Can't go over.
> Can't go under.
> Let's go through. (Act out walking through a jungle.)

Repeat:

> Going on a lion hunt. (Clapping)
> Going to catch a big one. (Clapping)
> STOP. (Stop)
>
> I see . . .

Include climbing in and out of a jeep, marching across hot sand (walk on tiptoes, on heels), climbing up and down a rope, walking through mud, swimming across a river, digging a trap, and paddling a canoe. Upon seeing the imaginary lion, the children freeze in a crouched position.

Children escape the lion by backtracking the sequence of actions. If space is limited, children can go through the actions standing in one place.

All ages can enjoy this. For older children, let them take turns narrating the story, or let some of them guess what is happening as other children perform the actions.

Teacher Observations

Body Awareness: Can the child maintain stationary postures by verbal cues, or does the child need to copy the teacher or other children?

Motor Planning: Can the child mimic postures easily?

99

London Bridge

Equipment

None.
(see music in appendix)

Activity

Children are divided into two groups. One group divides into pairs to form bridges and the other group forms a line which will pass under the bridges. The children who form the bridges can do so by standing, kneeling, or half-kneeling and holding hands, or sitting and joining feet. The children who pass under the bridge can walk, knee-walk, animal walk, hop, skip, or jump.

Song: London Bridge is falling down,
Falling down, falling down.
London Bridge is falling down
My fair lady.

Verses:

- Take the key and lock her up . . .
- Build it up with iron bars . . .
- Iron bars will bend and break . . .
- Build it up with silver and gold . . .

Teacher Observations

Motor Planning: Can the child adapt his movements to accommodate various size bridges?

Perception of Movement: Does the child have enough postural control to maintain positions?

Perception of Touch: Does the child avoid or over-react to the physical contact involved in this game?

Melt the Ice

Equipment

None.

Activity

Each child sits on the floor with knees bent, and arms hold the knees closely to the chest. The teacher says, "Hug your knees as tight as you can. Pretend you are an ice cube. The ice is slowly melting, slowly, slowly, slowly melting. You are melting into a nice big puddle on the floor."

Slowly, each body part relaxes onto the floor.

A darkened room promotes a more relaxed atmosphere with less distraction. This activity is especially helpful at the end of a motor session when children seem to be overactive and need to be calmed down for academics.

Teacher Observations

Body Awareness: Can the child stiffen all of body at one time to be an effective ice cube?

Motor Planning: Can the child relax just the one part of the body that is melting?

Mirror Image

Equipment

None.

Activity

Children pair off, facing one another. The teacher instructs the children to pretend that they are looking in a mirror. One child of each pair is designated the mirror. When the child who is not the mirror moves, the one who is the mirror must move in the same manner. Initially, it will help the children to learn the activity if the child doing the action does it in slow motion. The teacher may designate the activity if the children have difficulty getting started.

With small groups, the teacher may wish to have only one person doing the action and all of the others mirroring it. This variation enables the teacher to observe subtleties in performance.

To encourage children to be more precise in their mirroring, teams can be organized to perform and to judge accuracy of movement.

Teacher Observations

Body Awareness: Can the child maintain body postures without looking at his own body?

Motor Planning: Does the child mirror the action or attempt to reverse it?

Ocular Control: Is the child able to sustain visual contact in order to duplicate all of the action?

Pretzel

Equipment

None.

Activity

Children sit or stand in a line or a circle. They begin by pantomiming making pretzel dough. Next, they rub the dough all over themselves. Each child takes a turn being the baker and assumes a pretzel posture which all the others must imitate. The pretzel posture is chosen by the child. The posture may vary from a straight position to the arms crossing.

The children "bake" for twenty seconds (by holding still). After this the teacher and the "baker" test the children for "doneness" by gently pushing and pulling them. When testing for "doneness," give verbal cues such as "Make your arm very stiff so I can't move it." "Let's see if I can bend this pretzel." If any part moves, they must "bake" a little longer. When all are "done," the next child takes his turn assuming a new posture.

Teacher Observations

Body Awareness: Can the child hold a stationary posture?

Motor Planning: Can the child mimic postures or think up novel ones when it's his turn to be the "baker"?

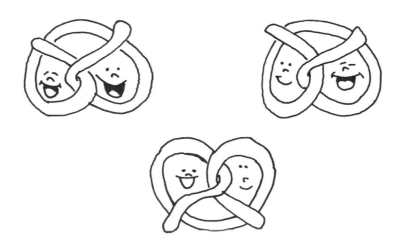

Progressive Aerobics

Equipment

None.

Activity

This game is similar to the game
I Packed My Grandmother's Suitcase.

The children stand in a circle. A designated child begins by saying, "I went to exercise class and I did *jumping jacks*" (exercise of child's choice). All children in circle demonstrate the action. The next child in the circle repeats the first action saying, "I went to exercise class and I did *jumping jacks* and *push-ups*" (demonstrating his choice of exercise). All children do movements as each exercise is named. This sequence continues until all children have had a turn to add to the list of exercises. Encourage each child during their turn to remember the preceding exercises before adding one of their own.

Teacher Observations

Auditory Processing: Can the child remember the sequence of exercises that preceded his turn?

Coordinating Body Sides: Can the child execute bilateral exercises smoothly?

Motor Planning: Do the movements resemble that of the stated exercise?

Perception of Movement: Can the child maintain balance and postural control for the various exercises?

Red Light, Green Light

Equipment   None.

Activity   Children line up along the starting line. If needed, starting and finish line may be made of masking tape or yarn. A leader stands at the finish line. Children progress according to a designated animal walk whenever leader says "green light." If child fails to stop when "red light" is called, then he must return to the starting line. If a child does not do the animal walk in the manner designated, then he must return to the starting line. When a child reaches the finish line, then he must progress backwards towards the starting line, again doing the designated animal walk.

Stop and go signs or color cards may be used. Start by giving children both an auditory and a visual cue; then see if they can attend to just a visual cue.

Teacher Observations

Auditory Processing: Can child control the impulse to move until he hears the appropriate verbal cue?

Body Awareness: Can the child stop on "red light"?

Motor Planning: Can the child quickly and smoothly assume various animal walk positions?

Red Rover

Equipment

None.

Activity

Children are divided into two groups and line up facing each other. Parallel start and finish lines, approximately fifteen feet apart, made of masking tape or yarn and a designated carpet square for each child to sit on may be used, if needed. The game is played much like traditional *Red Rover;* however, a specific movement pattern (variations of rolling, crawling, wheel-barrow walking, knee walking, animal walking, jumping, hopping, skipping) is called. For example, one team calls a child from the opposite team over: "Red Rover, Red Rover, send Cathy right over." This child moves in the designated manner over the line and sits with the new team. Cathy's team then calls another child over until every child has had a turn.

Teacher Observations

Motor Planning: Does child smoothly execute the pattern of movement he has been given?

Perception of Movement: Can the child maintain balance and move in a straight line while rolling, hopping, etc.?

Ring Around the Rosy

Equipment

None.
(see music in appendix)

Activity

Children hold hands and walk around in a circle as they chant.

Chant:
> Ring-around-the-rosy
> Pocket full of posies
> Ashes, ashes
> All fall down.

Verses:
- All clap hands
- All hop around
- All squat down
- All jump up and down
- All turn half-way around, etc.

Children follow the action suggested in the last portion of each verse.

Having the children hold hands and face outward from the circle is more challenging than facing the center. To add a creative component to this activity, have each child name an alternate action.

Teacher Observations

Auditory Processing: Does the child follow directions of the song?

Body Awareness: Is the child able to hold hands without dropping or squeezing other child's hand?

Perception of Movement: Is the child able to balance while performing all of the motor actions without dragging another child down?

Spinning Statue Freeze

Equipment

None.

Activity

Children pair off. The children grasp hands and spin around in a safe manner. It's usually best to have only one pair moving at a time. At the count of 1-2-3 they stop and assume a specific posture.

Suggested Postures

<u>Animals</u>
Elephant, donkey, rabbit, monkey, etc.
<u>Emotions</u>
Angry, happy, embarrassed, confused, frightened, surprised, etc.
<u>Reflections</u>
Child copies partner's or teacher's position.
<u>Robots</u>
Child holds posture. Teacher "activates the robot" by turning on one arm or leg at a time. The child maintains this action until every child has been activated.

Teacher Observations

Body Awareness: Can the child make body adjustments necessary to assume posture with ease and maintain the position?

Motor Planning: Can the child copy another person's posture?

Perception of Movement: Does the child overly seek or avoid spinning himself? This activity may not be appropriate for children who seem to get out of control by spinning themselves.

108

The Thousand Legged Worm

Equipment

None.
(see music in appendix)

Activity

Children sit or assume the "all-fours" position (on hands and knees). Space children so that everyone can see the leader. Children sing *The Thousand Legged Worm* to the tune *Polly-Wolly Doodle* as they copy the leader in moving specific body parts.

Song: Oh, the thousand legged worm
Oh, the thousand legged worm
Oh, the thousand legged worm
His head can turn.

Leader turns head from side to side.

Repeat song and substitute body parts:

Verses:
- His elbow can squirm . . .
- His fingers can squirm . . .
- His feet can turn . . .
- His tongue can squirm . . .
- His legs can turn . . .

Children may stomp their feet to keep the rhythm.

Teacher Observations

Auditory Processing: Is the child able to respond to auditory cues for following directions or does he depend on visual cues only?

Body Awareness: Does the child tend to tire easily while maintaining the all-fours posture?

Motor Planning: Can the child imitate movements of the leader

Perception of Movement: When in all-fours position, can the child maintain balance and posture while moving an arm or leg when he is on his hands and knees?

The Tortoise and the Hare

Equipment

None.

Activity

Space the children at arms length apart. If needed, floor markers can be used to maintain spacing. The main goal is to keep the children moving in place to increase overall endurance. Teacher tells the story of the tortoise (turtle) and the hare (rabbit). When speaking about the tortoise, the children must step in slow motion. When speaking about the hare, the children step quickly.

Storyline: The hare makes fun of the slow, clumsy tortoise. The tortoise then challenges the hair to a foot-race. The confident hare accepts the challenge. At the start of the race the hare sprints out of sight, leaving the tortoise to plod along. The hare gets tired from the fast pace and stops to rest. But the tortoise keeps plodding along. (Repeat the sprinting and plodding sequence several times.) The hare falls asleep thinking he has the race almost won. The tortoise wins because he keeps pacing himself and doesn't stop and get distracted from his goal of making it to the finish line.

When the children are comfortable with this, add interesting dilemmas to the story which require other movements.

Run with hands over head, on hips, on shoulders, across shoulders, waving, etc. The teacher can use instruments to maintain the tempo.

Especially good for rainy days. Keep this activity short, approximately 3 to 6 minutes. This activity can be calming or alerting, depending on the type of movements or storyline.

Teacher Observations

Auditory Processing: Does the child change his pace as the storyline varies?

Motor Planning: Can the child make appropriate changes in the tempo and in body positions?

We Waded In the Water

Equipment

None.
(see music in appendix)

Activity

Children sit or stand in a circle. To the tune of *The Battle Hymn of the Republic*, sing.

Song: We waded in the water, and we got our feet
    all wet
We waded in the water, and we got our feet
    all wet
We waded in the water, and we got our feet
    all wet
But we didn't get our (CLAP, CLAP) wet (CLAP),
    yet (CLAP).

Repeat verses adding the next level of anatomy: Ankles, knees, thighs, elbows, hands, etc. Child pats body part when it is mentioned in the song.

Last Verse:
We waded in the water and we finally got
    it wet . . .
We finally got our (CLAP) bathing suit (CLAP)
    wet.

This activity can be varied by using crepe paper streamers as the water. Some of the children wave them horizontally while other children stand in their path.

Teacher Observations

Body Awareness: Is the child able to identify body parts?

Perception of Touch: Does the child complain about or avoid this activity?

Does the child rub his arms or legs excessively after the initial tactile input?

Jump Rope Games
Primary Sensory and Motor Components
Challenged In Each Activity

	AUDITORY PROCESSING	BODY AWARENESS	COORDINATING BODY SIDES	FINE MOTOR	MOTOR PLANNING	OCULAR CONTROL	PERCEPTION OF MOVEMENT	PERCEPTION OF TOUCH	VISUAL-SPATIAL PERCEPTION
Pre-Jump Rope Games									
Tug Boat		X					X		
Stationary Rope			X		X		X		
High Water-Low Water			X		X		X		
Snake					X				X
Ocean Waves					X				X
Beginning Jump Rope Games									
Jump The Shot					X	X	X		
Lasso Jump	X				X				
Inside Outside					X		X		
Jump Rope									
Easy Overhead					X		X		
Blue Bells					X		X		
Individual Jump Rope			X		X				
Stunt Jump	X		X						
Advanced Jump Rope									
Eskimo Jump Rope					X				X
Cooperative Jump Rope					X				X
Multiple Jump Rope					X	X			
Egg Beater					X				X

112

Pre-Jump Rope Games

Equipment

Jump rope, 12-15 feet long — one per two to four children.

Activity

Tug Boat
A pair of children sit, kneel, half-kneel, or stand in a line opposite one another. Each child grasps a portion of the rope as in traditional tug-of-war. The children then pull with even pressure and move forward and backward while singing *row, row, row your boat.* The object is to maintain an even pressure on the rope as it is moved, and not to knock the opponent down.

Song: Row, row, row your boat
           Gently down the stream.
           Merrily, merrily, merrily, merrily
           Life is but a dream.

Teacher Observations

Body Awareness: Does the child perceive how hard to pull on the rope to keep it taut?

Perception of Movement: Is the child able to stabilize at shoulders and hips to maintain an upright position?

Pre-Jump Rope Games
— Continued —

Equipment

Jump rope, 12-15 feet long — one per four to six children.

Activity

Stationary Rope
Stretch out the rope in a straight line on the ground. The children start at one end of the rope and jump side to side over the rope to the other end. Have them try to jump forwards and backwards over the rope and continue down to the end.

High Water — Low Water
The rope is held in a stationary position by two people standing at each end. (Be sure that the rope is held loosely in the hands.) Each child attempts to jump over the rope. Alter the rope's height. Try it limbo style.

Teacher Observations

Motor Planning: Is the child able to jump backwards and sideways as well as forward?

Perception of Movement: Does the child lose his balance when jumping over the rope?

Coordinating Body Sides: Is the child able to jump with both feet at the same time?

Pre-Jump Rope Games
— Continued —

Equipment

Jump rope, 12-15 feet long — one per four to six children.

Activity

Snake
Two rope turners move rope back and forth to make a snake motion. The height and width of the moving snake can be altered.

Ocean Waves
Two rope turners make waves in the rope by moving their arms up and down. The children try to time it so as to jump over a low part of the wave.

Teacher Observations

Motor Planning: Does the child time his jump to coincide with the rope's position?

Visual-Spatial Perception: Does the child appear to perceive the correct height of the rope and jump accordingly?

Beginning Jump Rope Games

Equipment

Jump the shot — one per six to eight children. (see appendix)

Activity

Jump the Shot
Floor markers for each child are arranged in a circle. The teacher or a child squats in the center of the circle and spins the rope so that each child jumps the shot as it passes by them.

Teacher Observations

Motor Planning: Can the child time the movements in order to jump sequentially?

Ocular Control: Can the child watch the shot as it approaches?

Perception of Movement: Can the child maintain his balance when jumping?

Beginning Jump Rope Games
— Continued —

Equipment

Jump rope, 6 feet long — one per child.

Activity

Lasso Jump
The children each shorten their ropes by holding both ends together. The children then hold the ropes at their sides with the looped end touching the ground. The rope is twirled, using wrist action. As the rope hits the ground, the child jumps to help encourage good timing and rhythm for more advanced jump rope games.

Clue the children to bend their knees and jump each time they hear the rope hit the ground.

Teacher Observation

Motor Planning: Is the child able to initiate and maintain the twirling motion with the rope?

Auditory Processing: Is the child able to attend to the slapping sound of his own rope?

Beginning Jump Rope Games
— *Continued* —

Equipment

Jump rope — 12-15 feet long — per eight to ten children.

Activity

Inside Outside
Two children turn the rope in a consistent rhythmical manner. The remaining children form a line and run through the rope without letting the rope touch them.

Cue the children to begin running when they hear the rope touch the ground. It may be helpful to mark starting and stopping lines.

Teacher Observation

Motor Planning: Is the child able to time when to run through the rope without letting the rope touch?

Perception of Movement: Is the child able to make the necessary anticipatory body movements prior to running through the rope?

Jump Rope Games

Equipment

Jump rope — 12-15 feet long — one per four to six children.
Masking tape marker.

Activity

Easy Overhead
One child and one adult turn the rope in a full circle. Child jumping stands on marker placed on the floor at the middle of the rope. Child jumping is asked to stay on the marker.

To assist in proper timing, give verbal cues and encourage the child to watch the adult's turning arm. To ensure success, allow the child to pause after each jump, if necessary.

To the tune of *Bluebells, Cockle Shells*, two rope turners swing rope back and forth, but not overhead. Practice jumping in rhythm to the song and the swinging rope before expecting a child to jump overhead. When accuracy is established, turn the rope overhead to when the word "over" is sung.

Teacher Observations

Motor Planning: Is the child able to time his jumps to the auditory and visual cues of the turning rope?

Perception of Movement: Can the child maintain balance when jumping consecutively?

Jump Rope Games
— *Continued* —

Equipment

One jump rope per child (the length of the jump rope should reach from armpit to armpit).

Activity

Individual Jump Rope
Have each child hold the rope with one end in each hand. Check for proper length of rope. Excess rope can be wrapped around the hand. The rope should be touching the ground behind the feet.

The children swing the rope overhead, holding their arms out to their side, approximately waist high. Watch for a tendency to bring the arms to the midline of the body after a swing. This can cause tripping and prevent the child from being ready for the next swing. Begin by having each child turn the rope once, let it hit the feet and step over it. Progress to jumping over the rope without stopping. Cue the children to bend their knees and jump each time they hear the rope touch the the ground. Encourage the children to take a preparatory rebound bounce while the rope is overhead. Try jumping with both feet together or alternating the weight from one foot to another.

Teacher Observation

Coordinating Body Sides: Can the child coordinate both hands to swing the rope overhead?

Can the child coordinate the top and bottom half of his body to jump over the rope?

Motor Planning: Can the child time the jump to make consecutive jumps?

120

Jump Rope Games
— Continued —

Equipment

Jump rope — 12-15 feet long — one per six to eight children.

Activity

Stunt Jump
Two people turn the rope in a full circle. The child jumping is given a specific sequence of actions to perform while jumping. These may include such things as touching the ground, turning around, clapping hands, slapping knees or feet. Familiar jump rope rhymes may be incorporated. Other children may be asked to join the child who is jumping.

For the more advanced jumpers, running in and out may be added. To meet the needs of the whole class, it may be better to have the more advanced jumpers use individual jump ropes.

Teacher Observations

Auditory Processing: Can the child follow directions to the song and stay in rhythm?

Coordinating Body Sides: Can the child coordinate arms and feet together when turning the rope for himself?

Advanced Jump Rope Games

Equipment

Eskimo jump rope — one per six to eight children. (see appendix)

Activity

Eskimo Jump Rope
Appoint two people to be rope turners. The activity is played using a back and forth movement of the rope. Each child takes a turn trying to repetitively jump over the bundle attached to the center of the rope.

When the children become familiar with the activity, they can jump with the rope turned in a full circle.

Teacher Observations

Motor Planning: Is the child able to time his jump so he clears the bundle?

Visual-Spatial Perception: Is the child able to align his body so he is in the center of the arc as the rope is swung?

Advanced Jump Rope Games
— Continued —

Equipment

Jump rope — 12-15 feet long — one per six to eight children.

Activity

Cooperative Jump Rope

Two people turn the rope in a full circle. The children stand in a line. The first child in line runs in and begins to jump. After three consecutive jumps, the next child in line runs in and begins to jump along with the first child. After they have jumped three consecutive jumps, the next child in line joins them. After three consecutive jumps another child joins those already jumping. This continues as long as no one fails to jump rope. The activity begins again when the group jumping misses, starting with those who haven't had a turn.

Teacher Observations

Motor Planning: Is the child able to jump on the balls of his feet in a bouncing rhythmical pattern?

Visual-Spatial Perception: Is the child able to maintain proper spacing while jumping with another child?

Equipment

Two or more jump ropes, 12-15 feet long.

Activity

Multiple Jump Rope
Appoint two rope turners for each rope. The ropes are spaced ten to twelve feet apart. They are turned in full circle fashion, both hitting the floor simultaneously. Each child takes a turn running through the moving ropes.

To increase the difficulty, the child may stop to jump a designated number of times in each rope.

Teacher Observations

Motor Planning: Is the child able to continue running through the ropes without losing his momentum?

Ocular Control: Can the child visually track the ropes as they turn in order to successfully time his entrance?

Advanced Jump Rope Games
— Continued —

Equipment

Jump rope — 12-15 feet long — two per ten to twelve children.

Activity

Egg Beater
Four rope turners are designated. The ropes are held at right angles to one another. They are turned simultaneously so that they hit the ground together. The child jumping enters from the corner where both ropes are turning towards him. After jumping in the center several times, they exit from the opposite corner.

Teacher Observations

Motor Planning: Is the child able to correctly time when he enters the turning ropes? Are the rope turners successful in synchronizing the rope turning?

Visual-Spatial Perception: Is the child able to perceive the center of the crossed ropes?

Jump Rope Rhymes

Bluebells, Cockle Shells

Bluebells, cockle shells,
   Eevy, ivy, over.
(Rope is swung back and forth
until "over," then it goes full
circle.)

Bread and Butter

Bread and butter,
   Sugar and spice,
How many people
   Think I'm nice?
One, two, three . . .
(Continue counting

Cinderella

Cinderella dressed in yellow,
   Went downstairs to kiss her fellow
How many kisses did she get?
   One, two, three . . .
(Continue counting)

Cinderella dressed in lace,
   Went upstairs to powder her face
How many pounds did it take?
   One, two, three . . .

Cinderella dressed in red,
   Went downstairs to bake some bread
How many loaves did she bake?
   One, two, three . . .

Doggies

Bulldog, poodle, bow wow wow.
How many doggies have we now?
   One, two, three . . .

Jump Rope Rhymes
— Continued —

Down In the Valley

Down in the valley,
   Where the green grass grows
There sat (Child's name)
   As pretty as a rose;
She sang, she sang
   She sang so sweet,
Along came (Child's name)
   And kissed her on the cheek.
How many kisses did she get?
   One, two, three . . .
(Continue counting)

Dutch Girl

I'm a little Dutch Girl
   Dressed in blue;
And these are the things
   I like to do;
Salute to the Captain,
   Bow to the Queen,
And turn my back
   To the mean old king.

Engine Number Nine

Engine, engine Number Nine,
   Goin' down Chicago Line,
See it sparkle, see it shine,
   Engine, engine Number Nine.
If the train should jump the track
   Will I get my money back?
Yes, no, maybe so . . .
(The word that the jumper misses on
   is the answer..)

Grace, Grace, Dressed In Lace

Grace, Grace, dressed in lace,
   Went upstairs to powder her face.
How many boxes did she use?
   One, two, three . . .

Jump Rope Rhymes
— Continued —

Hoppity, Hop

Hoppity hop to the barber shop
   How many hops before I stop?
One, two, three . . .

I Came To a River

I came to a river,
   I couldn't get across.
I paid ten dollars
   For an old blind horse.
I jumped on its back
   And its bones went crack.

We all played the fiddle
   Till the boat came back.

The boat came back,
   We all jumped in.

The boat turned over,
   And we all fell out.

Ice Cream Soda

Ice cream soda, Delaware punch,
   Tell me the name of your honeybunch.
A, B, C, D, E . . .
(The letter on which the jumper misses
is the first letter of the honeybunch's
name.)

I Love Coffee

I love coffee,
   I love tea,
I want (Child's name)
   To come in with me.

Johnny Over the Ocean

Johnny over the ocean,
  Johnny over the sea,
Johnny broke a bottle
  And blamed it on me.
I told Ma,
  Ma told Pa,
Johnny got a spankin'
  So, Ha! Ha! Ha!
How many spankings did he get?
  One, two, three . . .
(Continue counting)

Keep the Kettle Boiling

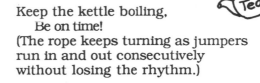

Keep the kettle boiling,
  Be on time!
(The rope keeps turning as jumpers
run in and out consecutively
without losing the rhythm.)

Lady, Lady

Lady, Lady at the gate,
  Eating cherries from a plate.
How many cherries did she eat?
  One, two, three . . .

Lady Bug, Lady Bug

Lady bug, lady bug turn around.
  Lady bug, lady bug, touch the ground.
Lady bug, lady bug, fly away home.
  Lady bug, lady bug, go upstairs.
Lady bug, lady bug, say your prayers.
  Lady bug, lady bug, turn out the light.
Lady bug, lady bug, say "Goodnight."

Jump Rope Rhymes
— Continued —

Mabel, Mabel

Mabel, Mabel, set the table,
    Just as fast as you are able.
And don't forget the RED HOT PEPPERS!
(Jump as fast as possible.)

Miss Lucy Had a Baby

Miss Lucy had a baby
(One child is jumping.)
    His name was Tiny Tim,
She put him in the bathtub
    To see if he could swim.
He drank up all the water,
    He ate up all the soap,
He tried to eat the bathtub,
    But it wouldn't go down his throat.
Miss Lucy called the doctor,
(Doctor runs in.)
    Miss Lucy called the nurse,
(Nurse runs in.)
Miss Lucy called the lady with
    the alligator purse.
(Lady runs in.)
"Mumps," said the doctor,
(All jump together.)
    "Measles," said the nurse,
"Nothing," said the lady with
    the alligator purse.
Out runs the doctor.
(Doctor runs out.)
    Out runs the nurse.
(Nurse runs out.)
Out runs Miss Lucy and the
    lady with the alligator purse.
(Lucy and lady run out.)

Jump Rope Rhymes
— Continued —

Mother, Mother, I Am Able

Mother, Mother, I am able
    To stand on a chair and set the table.
Daughter, daughter, don't forget
    Salt, vinegar, and red hot pepper!
(Regular jumping until "pepper.")

Polly Put the Kettle On

Polly put the kettle on
    And have a cup of tea.
In comes (Child's name)
    And out goes me!

Rooms For Rent

Rooms for rent
    Inquire within.
When I move out
    (Child's name) moves in

Snowman

Snowman, Snowman
    Big and round,
How many inches
    Are you around?
One, two, three . . .

Spanish Dancer

Not last night but the night before,
 Twenty-four robbers came knockin' at my door
As I ran out, they ran in,
(The jumper runs out, then in again)
 And this is what they said:
Spanish dancer, do the splits,
 Spanish dancer, do high kicks,
 Spanish dancer, touch the ground,
 Spanish dancer, run out of town.
(The jumper runs out.)

Teddy Bear

Teddy Bear, Teddy Bear,
 Turn around.
Teddy Bear, Teddy Bear,
 Touch the ground.
Teddy Bear, Teddy Bear,
 Show your shoe.
Teddy Bear, Teddy Bear,
 That will do!

Teddy Bear, Teddy Bear,
 Go upstairs.
Teddy Bear, Teddy Bear,
 Say your prayers.
Teddy Bear, Teddy Bear,
 Switch off the light.
Teddy Bear, Teddy Bear,
 Say goodnight.

Turkey, Turkey

Turkey, Turkey on the gate
 Let (Child's name) guess your weight
One, two, three . . .

Tool Activities
Primary Sensory and Motor Components
Challenged In Each Activity

	AUDITORY PROCESSING	BODY AWARENESS	COORDINATING BODY SIDES	FINE MOTOR	MOTOR PLANNING	OCULAR CONTROL	PERCEPTION OF MOVEMENT	PERCEPTION OF TOUCH	VISUAL-SPATIAL PERCEPTION
Cooking		X	X		X				
Finger Painting			X					X	
Folding Art			X						X
Play Dough				X				X	
Pop Beads				X					X
Rub Art		X		X					
Sewing Projects			X	X	X				
Shape Art					X				X
Spray Bottle Games				X		X			
Stamp Art		X		X					X
Sticker Art				X					X
Stringing				X				X	
Weaving			X	X					X

Cooking

Equipment

Appropriate cooking utensils.
Specific ingredients.

Activity

Choose a simple recipe that incorporates the
use of a variety of cooking utensils such as apple
slicer, egg separator or slicer, juicer, melon baller,
pancake turner, pastry tube, rolling pin, wire
whisk, etc.

When possible, separate the children into
small groups of two to four children with an
adult to assist. Demonstrate each step of the
recipe and allow each group to complete that
step before beginning the next.

Try the no-bake recipes displayed on the
following pages.

Teacher Observations

Coordinating Body Sides: Is the child able to
use one hand to stabilize the cooking utensil
while activating it with the other hand?

Motor Planning: Is the child able to effectively
use the specific cooking utensil?

Body Awareness: Can the child modulate the
correct amount of force needed to roll cookie
batter into balls? Is the child able to exert
sufficient strength to control a pastry tube?

No-Bake Recipes

Ants On A Log

Equipment	Vegetable brush
	Plastic knife

Ingredients	Celery
	Peanut butter
	Raisins

Clean the celery with a vegetable brush. Fill each celery stalk with peanut butter using a plastic knife. Place raisins in a row on top of the peanut butter.

Banana Bon Bons

Equipment	Nut grinder or chopper
	2-4 Plastic knives
	2 Soup bowls
	2 Plastic forks
	Platter

Ingredients	1 cup unsalted peanuts
	1 small jar of peanut butter
	4-6 firm bananas
	16 ounces flavored yogurt
	1 small package of coconut

Banana-Peanut Butter Bons

Grind nuts in a nut grinder and place in the bowl. Slice bananas into one-inch slices. Spread the banana slice with peanut butter until it is covered. Roll the peanut butter covered sliced banana in the nuts. Place it on the serving platter.

Banana-Coconut Bon Bons

Place the coconut into a bowl. Stir yogurt, spear banana slice and dip into yogurt to coat the slice completely. Roll the banana slice in the coconut and then place it on the platter.

No-Bake Recipes
— Continued —

Decorator Icing

Equipment	Small mixing bowl
	Egg beater
	Sifter
	Soup spoon
	Wax paper

Ingredients	3 egg whites
	1/2 teaspoon cream of tartar
	1 pound box powdered sugar

Separate eggs and place egg whites in a bowl. Sift cream of tarter and powdered sugar into the egg whites. Whip at high speed for 8 minutes until stiff peaks form. Cover icing and store at room temperature until ready to use. Icing can be used in a pastry tube to make small candy drops. Drops are placed on wax paper to dry. Candies can be used like stickers to decorate graham crackers. Use a dab of decorator icing to secure the dried candies.

Moon Balls

Equipment	Zip Lock plastic bag
	Rolling pin
	Medium size mixing bowl
	Soup bowl
	Spoon

Ingredients	Makes 20-30 1" balls
	1/2 cup honey
	1cup peanut butter
	1-1/2 cups powdered milk
	1-1/3 cups crushed cornflakes, branflakes, or other flake cereal

Place cornflakes into the Zip Lock bag and crush them by rolling with a rolling pin, or squeezing them by hand. Next, have the children put the first three ingredients into the mixing bowl and thoroughly mix it with their hands. Form this mixture into one inch balls and roll in the crushed flakes.

No Bake Recipes
— *Continued* —

Peanut Butter Date Balls

Equipment   Measuring cups
Grinder type nut chopper
Measuring spoon
Spoon

Ingredients   Makes 20-30 1" balls

1 cup extra chunky peanut butter
1 cup powdered sugar
1 cup chopped peanuts
1 cup chopped dates or raisins
1 tablespoon softened margarine

Mix all ingredients with hands; form into one inch balls.
Ready to eat.

Rice Cake Happy Faces

Equipment   Plastic knife

Ingredients   Rice cakes
Cream cheese
Raisins

Spread cream cheese onto rice cake using a plastic knife. Arrange raisins to form a happy face.

Finger Painting

Equipment

Finger paint paper.
Finger paint media:
      Liquid starch with tempera paint
      Shaving cream
      Instant pudding.
Aprons or shirts.

Activity

Have the children wear aprons or shirts to protect their clothes. Pour finger paint directly onto the table or finger paint paper.

Children can use both hands simultaneously to paint circles or simple patterns.

Patterns can be made by tapping individual fingers.

Have the children trace around their hand with the opposite index finger.

Grains such as rice, cornmeal, oatmeal, and lentils can be added to provide a variety of textures.

Prints can be made by laying newsprint over the child's painting and gently rubbing.

Teacher Observations

Coordinating Body Sides: Is the child able to make simultaneous mirrored movements with his hands?

Perception of Touch: Does the child avoid placing his hands into the paint?

Does the child frequently ask to wash his hands?

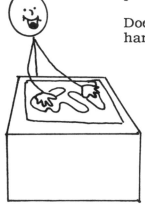

Folding Art

Equipment

Paper — or construction paper, typing paper, or wrapping paper.

Activity

The children are given pre-cut and pre-marked paper to fold. Until a child can fold with precision, stay with simple fan-folded projects such as inchworms, pop-outs, and accordion-legged animals and clowns.

Emphasize the necessity of folding carefully on the line and following the directions step by step. Dotted and solid lines may be used to designate inside and outside folds.

Teacher Observations

Coordinating Body Sides: Is the child able to coordinate both hands so as to manipulate paper for folding?

Visual-Spatial Perception: Is the child able to orient his paper correctly?

Playdough Activities

Equipment

Playdough.
Cookie cutters.
Cookie guns.
Egg slicers.
Garlic press.
Plastic drop cloth.
Plastic knives.
Plastic tubes (curlers).
Rolling pins.
Scissors.

Activity

Place a plastic drop cloth on the floor under the tables. Have the children sit, kneel, or stand at the table. Give each child some of the playdough and allow him to choose one or two utensils from the equipment list.

Make balls or eggs by rolling a piece of dough between the palms of the hands.

Make snakes by rolling a ball of dough back and forthwith the palm of the hands or by pressing dough through a plastic tube. Cut the dough snakes into discs with a plastic knife or scissors.

Roll the dough with a rolling pin. Cut flat dough with cookie cutters.

Press the dough through garlic press.

Press the dough into molds to make shapes.

Use a cookie gun or press to make individual shapes or snakes.

Cut the dough into slices with an egg slicer.

Teacher Observations

Fine Motor: Does the child have difficulty manipulating tools?

Perception of Touch: Does the child avoid putting his hands into playdough mixture?

140

Playdough Recipe

1 cup flour
1 teaspoon cream of tartar
1/2 cup salt
1 tablespoon oil
1 cup water
Food color
Scent (optional)

Mix all of the ingredients together. Heat over a very low heat, stirring constantly until the mixture begins to ball.

Continue to cook until the dough reaches the desired stiffness.

Turn out onto a floured surface and knead until it has cooled.

Store in an airtight container.

Pop Beads

Equipment

Pop beads — six per child.
Bucket of water.
Slotted spoon.
Trigger-type spray bottle.
Bean bags.

Activity

The children can try to duplicate pop bead designs according to color, shape, and sequence.

Pop beads can be used to measure objects in the room to compare various sizes and lengths.

Have the children connect pop beads to make various sized rings. Place the rings on the floor for targets. Have the children toss bean bags into the pop bead rings.

Individual pop beads can be used to toss into targets such as baskets, buckets, rings.

Float individual pop beads in a bucket of water. Have the children take turns fishing for pop beads with a slotted spoon.

Float individual pop beads in a bucket of water. Have the children take turns trying to propel a pop bead in the water by squirting at it with a spray bottle.

Teacher Observations

Fine Motor: Does the child have the strength and coordination to manipulate the pop beads and the spray bottle?

Visual-Spatial Perception: Is the child able to accurately measure objects and compare sizes with pop beads?

Is the child able to approximate the target when tossing bean bags or pop beads?

Rub Art

Equipment

Crayons, pencils, chalk.
Relief designs:

Leaves	Rubber bands
String	Paper shapes
Paper clips	Confetti

Dried glue relief drawings.
Paper.

Activity

The child places paper over an object to be trans-ferred and then rubs the flat side of the crayon over the paper until the impression of the design shows.

For variation, integrate this activity into a lesson on numbers, letters, spelling words, or math problems. Write the particular item on heavy cardboard with hot glue from a glue gun or withwhite school glue. When dry, have the child make a rubbing. The cardboard can be cut into smaller pieces. Numbers and math signs can be added to form equations.

Teacher Observations

Body Awareness: Is the child able to judge the amount of pressure needed to make the impression visible?

Fine Motor: Is the child able to securely hold the side of the crayon when he rubs the crayon across the paper?

Sewing Projects

Equipment

Yarn, shoelaces, string, thread.
Needles, bobby pins.
Paper, felt, material.
Hole punch.

Activity

Cut string into 12 to 18 inch pieces.
Tape the end of the yarn, loop a double
strand of yarn through a bobby pin or
thread a large-eyed needle.

Paper Packets
Staple together two pieces of construction paper
and mark three edges of the paper with spots to be
punched for holes. Have the children punch holes
on the designated spots if they are able to use the
hole punch. Sew together the three sides of the
paper packet, and remove the staples. Paper
packets can be made in a variety of shapes and sizes.

Felt and Button Projects
Buttons can be sewn onto felt to make projects
such as head bands and bracelets. The teacher
may want to pre-thread the needles so that the
thread is doubled and knotted on the end. The
child sews the buttons on a strip of felt and
secures them with a knot on the reverse side.
Attach the ends of the project together by sewing
a button on one end and cutting a small hole on
the other end.

Teacher Observations

Coordinating Body Sides: Can the child
stabilize the project with one hand and sew
with the other hand?

Fine Motor: Does the child have difficulty
manipulating the needle?

Motor Planning: Does the child have difficulty
sewing through the holes in the proper sequence?

Shape Art

Equipment

Paper:

Construction paper
Tissue paper
Wall paper
Wrapping paper.

Glue.

Activity

Give each child a piece of paper, glue, and a variety of geometric shapes. Choose from the following list according to ability.

Glue shapes onto paper, creating random designs.

Glue shapes onto pre-outlined designs.

Duplicate designs.

Experiment with the placement of shapes to create identifiable objects.

Formulate a plan describing verbally what they are going to create. Provide several examples when giving directions, but do not allow the children to copy directly.

Teacher Observations

Motor Planning: Can the child formulate a plan and follow through with his plan?

Visual-Spatial: Can the child accurately match designs with his paper shapes?

Can the child create identifiable objects?

Spray Bottle Games

Equipment

Trigger-handled spray bottles.
Bucket of water for refilling bottles.
Targets:
        Playground cement
        Beach ball with shaving cream
        Bubbles
        Ping pong balls.

Activity

The children line up in groups of two or three and each group is given one spray bottle.

Children can draw letters and numbers on cement using a stream of water from the spray bottle.

A beach ball can be placed on top of the bucket four to six feet from the children. Draw a happy face, number, or letter on the ball with shaving cream and have the children take turns squirting the water at the beach ball until the soap is washed off.

Children can spray a stream of water to pop bubbles blown by the teacher.

Children can have relay races propelling a ping pong ball with a stream of water over a designated finish line.

Teacher Observations

Fine Motor: Is the child able to repeatedly squeeze the spray bottle trigger?

Ocular Control: Does the child maintain visual contact with the object that he is spraying with water?

Stamp Art

Equipment

Stamps:

    Fingers, hands, toes, feet
    Halved potatoes, apples, oranges,
      lemons
    Sponges
    Blocks of wood or dowels with rubber
      designs on the bottom
    Pencils with unused eraser tips.

Paper:

    Newsprint
    Butcher paper
    Computer paper
    Quadrille paper.

Ink:

    Water base ink pads
    Tempera paint
    Acrylic paint.

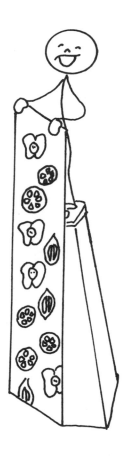

Activity

Have the children:

Use stamps to repeat random designs on large pieces of paper.

Duplicate specific designs.

Copy precise designs on quadrille paper.

Teacher Observations

Body Awareness: Does the child push too hard or too soft with the stamp?

Fine Motor: Is the child able to maintain a consistent grasp on the stamp to make a complete impression?

Visual-Spatial Perception: Can the child space the stamp designs accurately when precision is required?

Sticker Art

Equipment

Stickers.
Sticker design samples.
Wax paper.

Activity

Children may choose a design and outline the design with sticker dots.

The children can place stickers on a picture to match appropriate shapes.

Duplicate simple designs or practice number concepts printed on graph paper. The children are then asked to position the stickers accurately within the lines.

Wax paper can be placed over sticker projects so that designs can be used over again.

Teacher Observations

Fine Motor: Does the child have adequate fine grasp to pick up stickers, using thumb and index finger?

Visual-Spatial Perception: Can the child place stickers in the correct position on his paper?

Stringing

Equipment

String, thread, or yarn — 24 inches long.
Needles or tape.
Scissors.
Stringable objects:

Cereal	Playdough beads	Beads
Cranberries	Marshmallows	Straws
Macaroni	Paper shapes	Sequins
Buttons		

Activity

Tie a knot in one end of the string. Use a needle or tape on the other end. Provide appropriate supplies for one of the following activities:

Colored Straw Necklace — Have the children cut colored straws into pieces approximately 1/2 to 1 inch long. String the pieces to form a necklace.

Paper Shape Necklace — The teacher marks a spot on each shape where the hole is to be made. Using the paper punch, the children then punch the holes. Hole reinforcers can be used to prevent the holes from tearing. Intersperse paper shapes with other stringable objects such as cut straws.

Confetti Necklace — The children can use a needle and thread to string confetti made from the hole punch.

Playdough Beads — Have the children roll out playdough snakes. The snakes are then cut into 1/2 inch pieces. A toothpick is used to poke a hole into the center. Let the playdough dry and then string the beads.

Painted Salad Macaroni — The children can paint macaroni pieces with tempera paint. Let them dry and then string them.

Teacher Observations

Fine Motor: Does the child have any difficulty using the tools such as scissors and the hole punch?

Perception of Touch: Is the child resistive to using any of the materials?

Weaving

Equipment

Construction paper — two per child, scissors, paste or glue.

Activity

Cut the construction paper in the desired shape, i.e., heart, shamrock, triangle. Fold the paper in half and mark a one-inch margin at the open end. Make straight cuts from the fold to the margin approximately one inch apart. This is the warp.

Cut the second piece of construction paper lengthwise into half-inch wide strips. This is the weft.

Weave a strip of paper over then under the warp. Weave the second strip next to the first, starting under then over. Repeat this process, continuing to alternate the over and under pattern. When the entire warp is filled with strips, trim the excess and glue the ends to secure.

As the children become more adept at weaving, variations in the patterns can be made by skipping one or more spaces on the warp, changing colors, or using variousmaterials for the weft.

Teacher Observations

Coordinating Body Sides: Is the child able to use both hands together to manipulate the materials with ease?

Fine Motor: Does the child have good finger dexterity?

Visual-Spatial Perception: Is the child able to repeat the designated pattern with each strip woven?

Appendix

Bean Bags

Materials   Heavy broadcloth, canvas, denim, corduroy. Pinto beans, rice, popcorn.

Directions

1) Cut fabric: 10" X 5" for small bean bags; 10" X 20" for large bean bags (Figure 1).

2) Fold fabric in half with right sides together and stitch half-inch seams (Figure 2).

3) Turn bean bags right side out. Press unstitched edge under half-inch.

4) Top stitch around bean bag, leaving a hole large enough for a funnel (Figure 3).

5) Fill bean bags. Approximately one cup per small bean bag; three cups per large bean bag.

6) Top stitch over the filling hole.

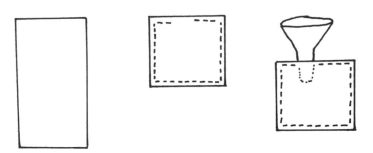

Figure 1   Figure 2   Figure 3

Bleach Bottle Scoop

Materials   Clean bleach bottle.
9" dowel or piece of wood to fit the handle of
the bleach bottle.
Cloth tape.

Directions

1)   Cut the bottom of the bottle out on a
diagonal.

2)   Insert the dowel or board into the
handle.

3)   Secure the handle with cloth tape.

Eskimo Jump Rope

Materials

One jump rope, 12-15 feet long.
One king-sized pillowcase.
Plastic or cloth tape.
Newspaper.

Directions

1) Make a 2" slit in the center of the sewn end of the pillowcase.

2) Center the pillowcase along the length of the rope.

3) Bunch the sewn end of the pillow-case tightly around the rope and secure with tape. (Extend the tape 2-3 inches beyond the pillowcase.)

4) Fill the pillowcase with crumpled newspaper.

5) Bunch the open end of the pillowcase and secure it with tape.

6) Tie a loop at each end of the rope to form handles.

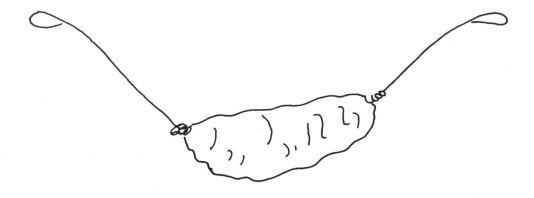

Jump the Shot Rope

Materials

One-half pound bean bag.
One six-foot jump rope.
Thread and needle.

Directions

1) Make a 2" slit in the stitched seam along the edge of the bean bag.

2) Tie a double knot in one end of the jump rope.

3) Poke the knot through the slit in the bean bag.

4) Triple stitch the bean bag to resecure the opened seam.

5) Tie a looped handle on the other end of the jump rope.

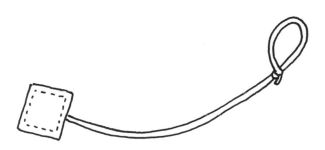

Lummi Sticks

Materials

Wooden dowels.
(Recommended sizes: 1/2", 3/4", 1")
Permanent marking pens.

Directions:

1)   Cut two 36-inch dowels into three 12-inch lengths.

2)   Sand the edges.

3)   Color the tips of each pair with the permanent marking pens for ease in sorting and for variation in game playing.

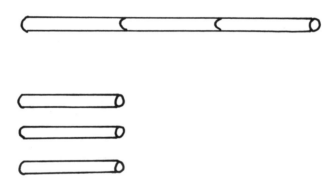

Streamers

Materials

One 2" X 60" strip of crepe paper or spinnaker cloth per streamer.
One popsicle stick per streamer.
Newspaper.
Cloth tape.

Directions

1) Fold the strip in half and attach the folded end to a popsicle stick with the cloth tape.

2) Fold a single sheet of newspaper into a 4-1/2 inch strip.

3) Roll the strip of newspaper tightly around the popsicle stick and secure with tape.

4) Wrap the tape around the entire newspaper handle.

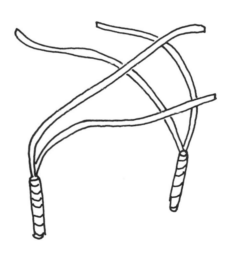

Two-Handed Bat

Materials

Two 2-liter plastic soda pop bottles per bat.
Crumpled newspaper.
Cloth tape.

Directions

1) Cut the bottom three inches off the bottles (Figure 1).

2) Cut notches two inches deep around the bottom of one bottle (Figure 2).

3) Fill both bottles with the crumpled newspaper.

4) Insert the bottom of the bottle with the notched edge into the bottom of the other bottle.

5) Wrap tape around the seam where the bottles join (Figure 3).

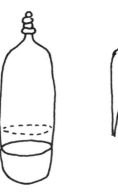

Figure 1

Figure 2

Figure 3

Weighted Plastic Pop Bottles

Materials   One 1-liter plastic soda pop bottle.
                   Pinto beans — one-half pound per bottle.
                   Cloth tape.

Directions

1)   Pour half a pound of pinto beans into a clean bottle.

2)   Replace the cap and seal it with cloth tape.

Weighted Snake

Materials
One 10" X 38" piece of heavy cotton fabric.
Three pounds of pinto beans.

Directions

1) Fold the fabric in half lengthwise and stitch along the raw edge, leaving an opening large enough to turn the fabric right side out.

2) Turn the fabric right side out and stitch around the edges to make a 1/2 inch reinforced border.

3) Fill the tube loosely with the pinto beans and stitch the opening closed.

4) Distribute the beans within the tube into three sections and stitch two vertical lines as shown on the illustration.

5) Draw or applique a face on one end of the snake.

Wiffle Ball Catcher

Materials

One 2-liter plastic soda pop bottle.
One 2-3/4" Wiffle ball.
One 30 inch piece of kite string.

Directions

1) Cut off the bottom of the bottle,
    leaving a 7 inch bowl. (Figure 1)

2) Attach one end of the string to the
    Wiffle ball. (Figure 2)

3) Attach the other end of the string
    to the neck of the bottle (Figure 2).

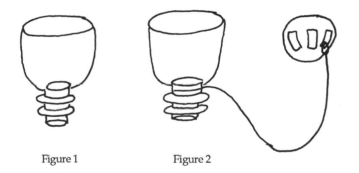

Figure 1   Figure 2

Writing Paper

Grade K-1

Grade 2

Grade 3
cursive

Grade 4-6
cursive

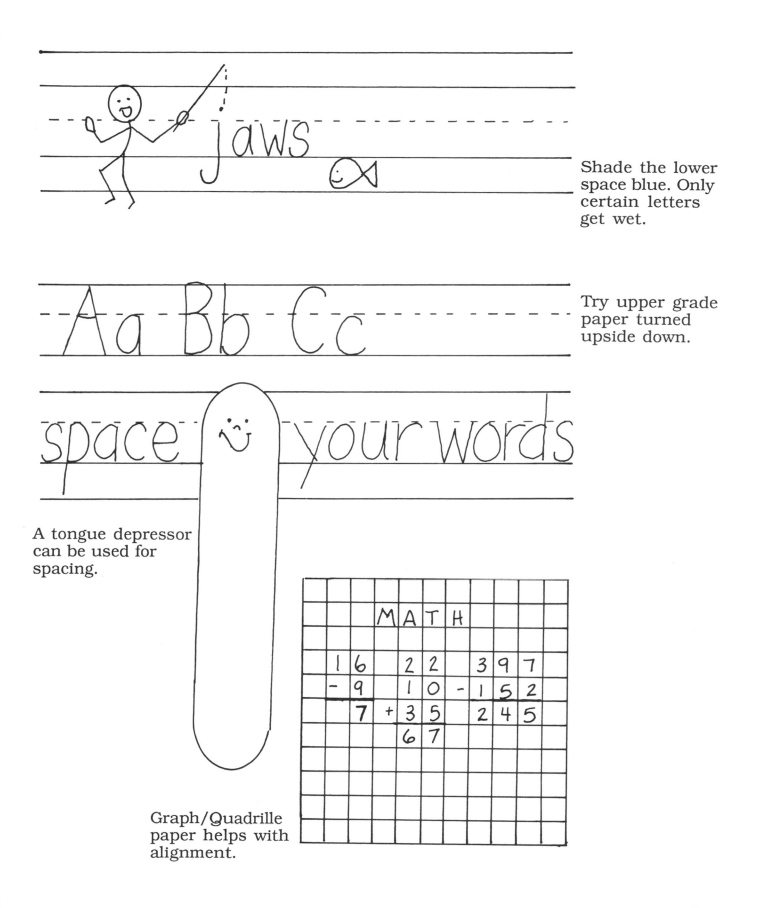

jaws

Shade the lower space blue. Only certain letters get wet.

Aa Bb Cc

Try upper grade paper turned upside down.

space your words

A tongue depressor can be used for spacing.

MATH

		M	A	T	H			
1	6		2	2		3	9	7
−	9		1	0		− 1	5	2
	7	+	3	5		2	4	5
			6	7				

Graph/Quadrille paper helps with alignment.

A Sailor Went To Sea

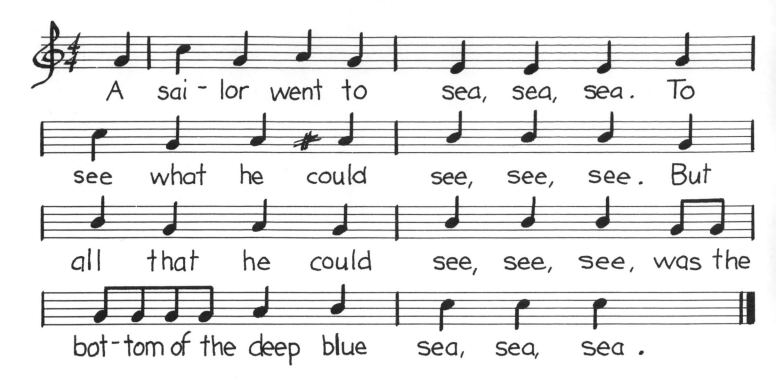

A sai-lor went to sea, sea, sea. To
see what he could see, see, see. But
all that he could see, see, see, was the
bot-tom of the deep blue sea, sea, sea.

A-Tisket, A-Tasket

A-tis-ket, a-tas-ket, a green and yel-low
bas-ket, I wrote a let-ter to my love and
on the way I dropped it. I dropped it, I
dropped it, and on the way I dropped it, A
lit-tle boy girl picked it up and put it in his her

pock-et.

Bingo

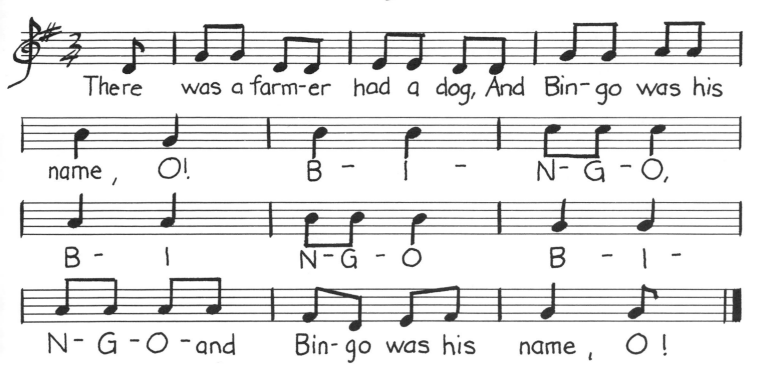

There was a farm-er had a dog, And Bin-go was his name, O! B - I - N-G -O, B - I N-G - O B - I - N- G -O -and Bin-go was his name, O!

Hambone

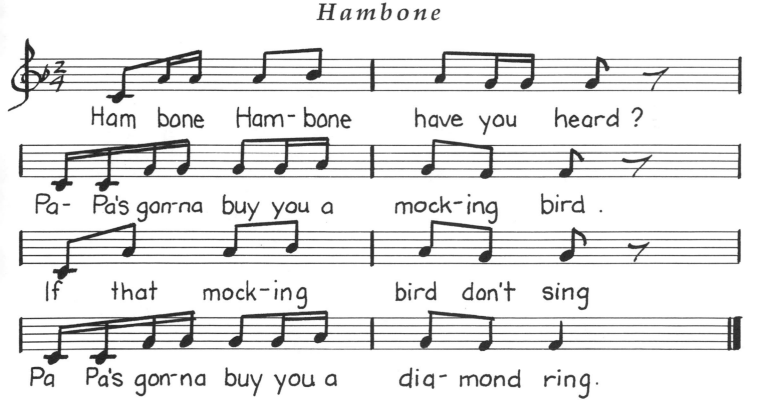

Ham bone Ham-bone have you heard? Pa- Pa's gon-na buy you a mock-ing bird. If that mock-ing bird don't sing Pa Pa's gon-na buy you a dia-mond ring.

Head and Shoulders

Head and shoul-ders, knees and toes, knees and toes

Head and shoul-ders, knees and toes, knees and toe - - - - - s.

Eyes and ears and mouth and nose,

Head and shoul-ders, knees and toes, knees and toes.

Hokey Pokey

You put your right hand in. You put your right hand out. You put your

right hand in and you shake it all a-bout. You

do the ho-key-po-key and you turn your-self a - bout.

That's what it's all a - bout.

Jimmy Crack Corn

Jim-my crack corn and I don't care,
Jim-my crack corn and I don't care,
Jim-my crack corn and I don't care, My
mas-ter's gone a - way.

Johnny Pounds With One Hammer

John-ny pounds with one ham-mer, one ham-mer
one ham-mer, John-ny pounds with one ham-mer
now he pounds with two.

167

London Bridge

Lon-don Bridge is fal-ling down, fal-ling down,
fal-ling down, Lon-don Bridge is fal-ling down,
my fair la - dy.

Long Legged Sailor

Have you ev-er, ev-er, ev-er in your long leg-ged life seen a
long leg-ged sai-lor and his long leg-ged wife ?

Miss Lucy Had A Baby

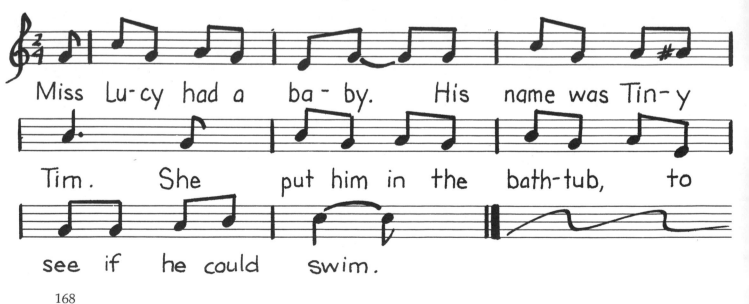

Miss Lu-cy had a ba-by. His name was Tin-y
Tim. She put him in the bath-tub, to
see if he could swim.

168

Miss Mary Mack

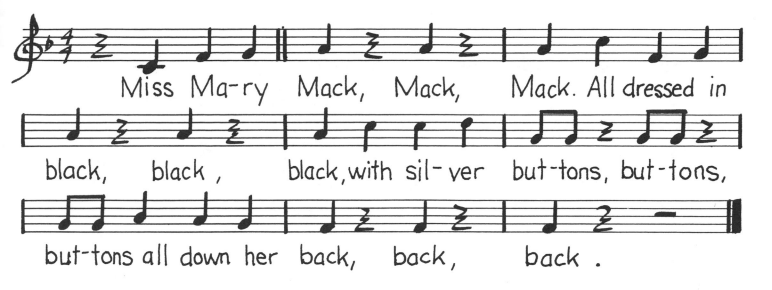

Playmate

Pop! Goes The Weasel

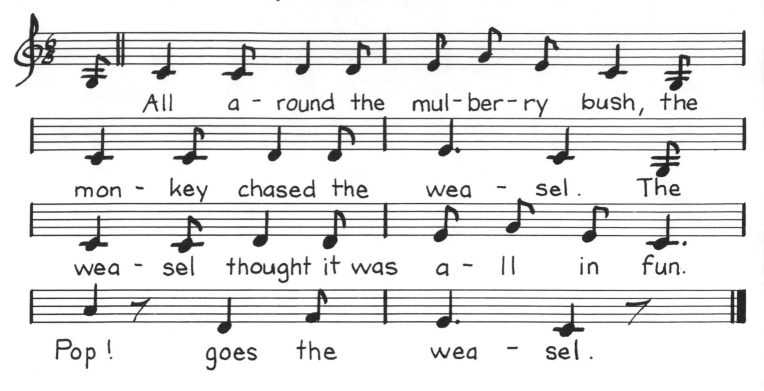

All a-round the mul-ber-ry bush, the
mon-key chased the wea-sel. The
wea-sel thought it was a-ll in fun.
Pop! goes the wea-sel.

Pretty Little Dutch Girl

I am a pret-ty lit-tle Dutch girl as
pret-ty as I can be. And
all the boys in the neigh-bor-hood are
cra-zy o-ver me.

Ring Around The Rosey

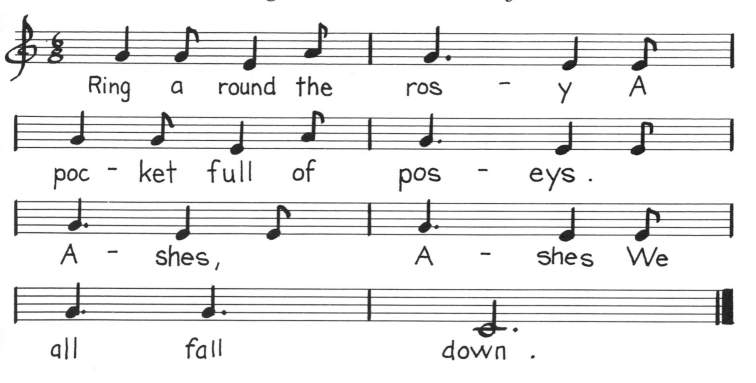

Row, Row, Row Your Boat

Skida Marink

Ten Little Indians

One lit-tle, two lit-tle three lit-tle In-dians;
four lit-tle, five lit-tle, six lit-tle In-dians;
seven lit-tle, eight lit-tle, nine lit-tle In-dians
ten lit-tle In-dian boys.

The Bear Went Over The Mountain

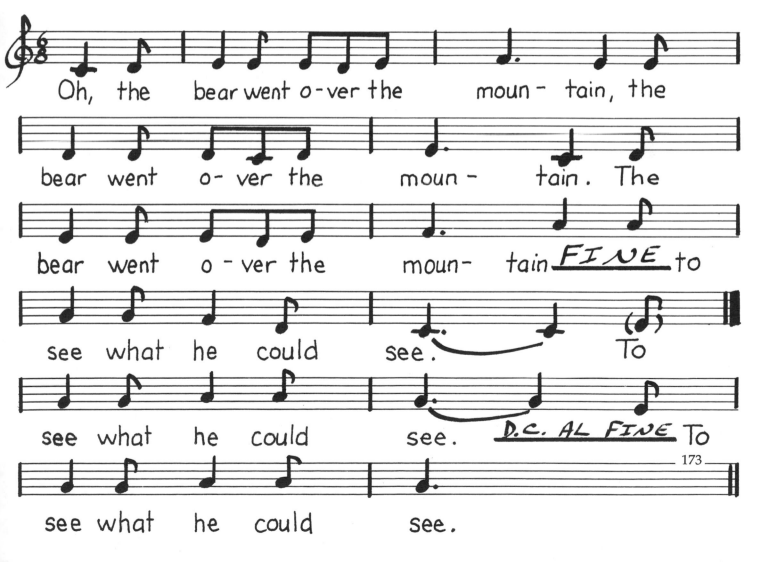

Oh, the bear went o-ver the moun-tain, the
bear went o-ver the moun-tain. The
bear went o-ver the moun-tain *FINE* to
see what he could see. To
see what he could see. *D.C. AL FINE* To
see what he could see.

173

The Thousand Legged Worm

This Old Man

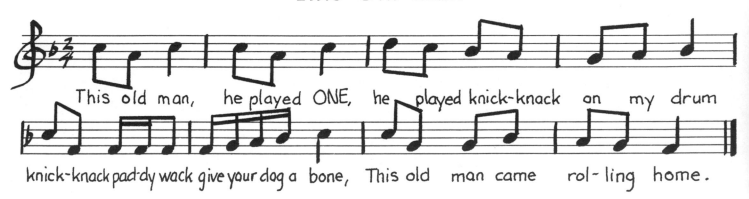

We Waded In The Water

We wa-ded in the wa-ter, and we got our feet all wet. We wa-ded in the wa-ter, and we got our feet all wet. We wa-ded in the wa-ter and we got our feet all wet. But we didn't get our ank — les wet yet.

Bibliography

Bibliography

Ayres, A. Jean, *Developmental Dyspraxia and Adult Onset Apraxia,* Torrance, California: Sensory Integration International, 1985.

Ayres, A. Jean, *Sensory Integration and the Child,* Beverly Hills, California: Western Psychological Services, 1979.

Banus, Barbara S., *The Developmental Therapist: A prototype of the pediatric occupational therapist,* Thorofare, New Jersey: Charles B. Slack, Inc., 1979.

Beall, Pamela C. and Nipp, Susan H., *Wee Sing and Play,* Los Angeles, California: Price/Stern/Sloan, 1982.

Centralia School District, *Primary Physical Education,* Buena Park, California: Duplicated by Orange County Department of Education 372217, 1973.

DeQueirios, Julio B. and Schrager, Orlando L., *Neuropsychological Fundamentals In Learning Disabilities,* San Rafael, California: Academic Therapy Publications, 1978.

Orlick, Terry, *The Cooperative Sports & Games Book,* New York: Pantheon Books, 1978.

Orlich, Terry, *The Second Cooperative Sports & Games Book,* New York: Pantheon Books, 1982.

Rasmussen, Richard M. and Rasmussen, Ronda L., *The Kids Encyclopedia of Things to Make and Do,* San Diego, California: Oak Tree Publications, Inc., 1981

Ventura County Special Education Service Area Consortium, *Motor Program Handbook: A guide for teachers,* Ventura, California, September, 1983.

Wirth, Marian J., *Teacher's Handbook of Children's Games: A guide to developing perceptual-motor skills,* West Nyack, New York: Parker Publishing Co., Inc., 1976.